The Gentrification of the Mind

The Gentrification
of the Mind

Witness to a Lost Imagination

Sarah Schulman

UNIVERSITY OF CALIFORNIA PRESS

Berkeley   Los Angeles   London

University of California Press, one of the most distinguished university presses in the United States, enriches lives around the world by advancing scholarship in the humanities, social sciences, and natural sciences. Its activities are supported by the UC Press Foundation and by philanthropic contributions from individuals and institutions. For more information, visit www.ucpress.edu.

University of California Press
Berkeley and Los Angeles, California

University of California Press, Ltd.
London, England

First paperback printing 2013

Library of Congress Cataloging-in-Publication Data

Schulman, Sarah, 1958–
    The gentrification of the mind : witness to a lost imagination/Sarah Schulman.
       p.   cm.
    ISBN 978-0-520-28006-9 (pbk : alk. paper)
    1. AIDS (Disease)—Social aspects.   2. AIDS (Disease)—United States.
3. Gentrification—United States.   4. Urban renewal—United States.
5. Urbanization—United States.   I. Title.
    RA644.A25S363 2012
    362.196′9792—dc23

                                                                      2011018311

Manufactured in the United States of America

21   20   19   18   17   16   15   14   13
10   9   8   7   6   5   4   3   2

In keeping with a commitment to support environmentally responsible and sustainable printing practices, UC Press has printed this book on Rolland Enviro100, a 100% post-consumer fiber paper that is FSC certified, deinked, processed chlorine-free, and manufactured with renewable biogas energy. It is acid-free and EcoLogo certified.

To Jim Hubbard
Thank you for being accountable, keeping your
promises, and being willing to face and deal with
problems regardless of their complexity.

CONTENTS

ACKNOWLEDGMENTS

This book was written with support from The Virginia Colony for the Creative Arts, Ledig House, and The Norman Mailer Writers Colony.

Thanks to my friends from the neighborhood, especially those of you on Ninth Street who have trod this path with me these many years. Special thanks to Dudley Saunders for reading and to Jack Waters, Peter Cramer, Bina Sharif, Kathy Danger, and the other survivors of AIDS and gentrification with whom I share this city.

Making Record from Memory

> The first step in liquidating a people ... is to erase
> its memory. Destroy its books, its culture, its history.
> Then have somebody write new books, manufacture
> a new culture, invent a new history. Before long the
> nation will begin to forget what it is and what it was.
> The world around it will forget even faster.
>
> Milan Kundera

It's 2001. I am in Los Angeles trying to break into film or television. It's been a tough day. I had a "meeting" with a film producer/agent/manager that was not encouraging. In New York, people have meetings because they have something to accomplish together. They need to sit down and work out the details, or else they are hoping to find a place in each other's lives: as lovers, collaborators, friends. But LA is different. People have meetings so that, if one of them should ever become famous in the future, the other will have "met" them. I know this because my friend Dudley, transplanted from the East Village to West Hollywood, lent me his copy of the Hollywood primer *Hello, He Lied* by Linda Obst so that I can be prepared for these strange rituals of nothingness.

"So, what novelist are your novels most like?" she asks.

I'm stymied. This is not a question that novelists ask ourselves, since the goal is to have something intimate and specific about our voices. *Think, Sarah, quick.* My mind is spinning. *Think of someone she may have heard of.*

"Uhm. Philip Roth?"

"I'm sorry," she said. "I'm not familiar with him."

Later I'm driving home in my white rental car, knowing I should have said "John Grisham." I hate myself. I'm an idiot. No matter how much I dumb down, it is never dumb enough. I flip through the radio stations, determined to learn the latest hits and become more in tune with the pop culture I'm trying to penetrate but bored to tears, end up settling on NPR. Bizarrely, this very day is the twentieth anniversary of AIDS. Decontextualized by palm trees, I listen. The announcer is discussing events that I know intimately, organically, that have seared the emotional foundation of my adult life. And yet there is a strangely mellow tone to the story. It's been slightly banalized, homogenized.

This is the first time I've heard AIDS being historicized, and there is something clean-cut about this telling, something wrong. Something . . . gentrified.

"At first America had trouble with People with AIDS," the announcer says in that falsely conversational tone, intended to be reassuring about apocalyptic things. "But then, they came around."

I almost crash the car.

Oh no, I think. *Now this.* Now after all this death and all this pain and all this unbearable truth about persecution, suffering, and the indifference of the protected, *Now,* they're going to pretend that *naturally, normally* things just *happened* to get better.

That's the way we nice Americans naturally are. We *come around* when it's the right thing to do. We're so nice. Everything just happens the way it should.

This? I realize the way one realizes that the oncoming train is unavoidable and I'm stuck on the track. *This is going to be the official history of AIDS?*

I pull the car over, whip out my brand-new first cell phone, and call Jim Hubbard in New York. We have to do something, *right now.* In 1986 Jim and I cofounded the New York Lesbian and Gay Experimental Film Festival (now known as MIX, and approaching its twenty-fifth year). Building a community institution with someone is a very bonding experience, and I know that together we can find a way to change this distortion of AIDS history. Jim is on it immediately. We cannot let the committed battle of thousands of people, many to their deaths, be falsely naturalized into America "coming around." No one with power in America "comes around." They always have to be forced into positive change. But in this case, many of the people who forced them are dead. The ones who have survived are in a kind of hell of confusion and chaos that feels personal but is actually political, whether they have "moved on" and "are living their lives" or are confused, displaced, lost. We have responsibilities, after all, we the living.

"Ok," he says. And then it begins. The investigation.

Cut ahead to October 2010. For the past nine years Jim and I have been codirecting the ACT UP Oral History Project. We have conducted 128 long form (two- to four-hour) interviews with surviving members of ACT UP, New York (AIDS Coalition to Unleash Power). And we have a waiting list of one hundred more to go. We have a website (www.actuporalhistory.org)

where we post five minutes of streaming video of each interview and where viewers can download the entirety of each transcript for free. To date over eighty thousand people have downloaded these transcripts, many from Eastern Europe and Asia. We assume they are people with AIDS, in countries with no AIDS activist movement, who are looking for information. Jim has preserved two thousand hours of archival footage, which we have made available for free at the New York Public Library. Jim is now making a feature-length documentary, *United in Anger: A History of ACT UP*, which I am coproducing, and which will have its world premiere in 2012. I have been traveling the country showing excerpts of the film at colleges and universities, trying to get professors and graduate students to use the ACT UP Oral History Project in their research. Now, after almost a decade of intensive labor, the first books and dissertations using the interviews are starting to appear. Somehow, more personally important than all of the above is that Jim and I now have more cumulative information about ACT UP than anyone. After each interview we reconceptualize the project, we try to articulate a trajectory, we put together the pieces of what made the organization work and the consequences and impact of its actions on AIDS and on the world. We get ACT UP. And the more I understand what ACT UP was, the more I see what is missing from the contemporary discourse.

In 2008, Helen Molesworth, the lesbian genius curator who—at the time—was at the Harvard Art Museum, called us out of the blue and asked to show our interviews at the university's Carpenter Center. She put together an exquisite program of talks, discussions, films, and visual work and created a viewing room, set up a bit like an ACT UP meeting. One enters and sees many monitors, with faces, all within view of each other, but also private, and on each monitor is a loop of our interviews. The viewer selects a face, someone they'd like to meet, and then sits down before the monitor, puts on the headphones and listens to that ACT UPer tell their story. The show was such a success that it traveled to the White Columns gallery in Manhattan. And this October night in question, in 2010, was the opening.

It was an incredible night. Hundreds of people overflowing onto the sidewalk. It was a gathering of the remnants of the ACT UP tribe and people showed up in full force. But there also was a significant showing of a new element, lots of queer people in their twenties. Many were artists or students, who clearly had come to honor ACT UP. I stood back and looked from one group to the next. The ACT UPers, now in our fifties and sixties, had a ragged edge to us in some ways. And it was illuminating to see us gathered together in once place for the first time in so long. A lot of us had had real troubles, that was clear. Drug problems, problems of purpose, significant health problems—many of these guys had been on really rough medication combinations with horrible side effects. Many had significant facial wasting and their faces had sunken. Everyone had suffered profoundly from that magic combination of the mass death of their friends and the mass indifference of government, families, and society. We were laughing and smiling and hugging and flirting, as we always had with each other, but somehow it was being among each other that was the most normalizing. I looked at my friends from ACT UP and I saw people who were somehow both heroes and freaks, because they had achieved the impossible and paid the high price of alienation brought by knowledge, as heroes and freaks always do.

Happy to be part of it, and standing at an admiring distance were the younger people. Also hanging out, talking, flirting, happy, excited, but the two worlds were not mixing. Before me I saw two distinctly different experiences, separated by the gulf of action fueled by suffering on one hand, and the threat of pacifying assimilation on the other. When the ACT UPers were in *their* twenties, they were dying. And the replacements for the dead, these young, were on the road to normalcy. The young had the choice to live quietly because of the bold fury of the old. In the rare cases when the old have done the right thing, this is as it should be. And somehow, the presence of the young showed that they understood this, that someone had done something right and yet *these* ones were curious, attracted, intrigued by the potential of living for more than LGBT domesticity as their fate. Maybe they too would like to change the world.

Some weeks later I went out with six young queer artists to have a drink. One was just about to publish a book with a mainstream publisher and go on a book tour. One was preparing a show for a popular commercial venue. One was about to have a funded workshop for a piece he had written. They all seemed to be doing very well, having opportunities and fitting in to the cultural structure. When I asked one guy what he did for a living, he said "performance." I now know that that is code for "inherited wealth" and does not mean he earns his living as go-go dancer at the Pyramid Club to pay his $150 rent, as it would have in 1979. None were waiters, hustlers, legal proofreaders. One worked for a fancy art magazine, another was the assistant to a famous artist. They were American aristocracy —good suburbs and good schools, clean-cut homosexuals —but somehow still attracted to justice. As the evening progressed they started to express a reasonable discomfort with the ACT UPers. It was obvious that there was a wall between the two groups, and I guess we all wanted to understand what that was. The younger people loved ACT UP. But in some fundamental way they couldn't relate to it. They didn't understand what we had experienced. They had never been that oppressed. They had never been that profoundly oppressed. And yet, they wanted to relate. They also had never been that inspired, that inventive or that effective. They were intelligent and thoughtful. They wanted to understand.

"Why?" I asked. "What is it that you want to know?"

"I wonder what it means about me."

I wasn't sure if that was a suburban narcissism in which one has to be able to "identify" in order to internalize value *or* if they were doing the hard work of reaching out to connect with their own history. I also wanted them to be able to relate. And while I understand that they have never known mass death of their world, one of my fears for younger gay people, especially artists, is that they don't see how rigidly the marginalization of point of view is enforced in our own shared contemporary moment. Unlike my generation, who were told we were despised, they are told that things are better than they are. And they have to go through the difficult process of learning to realistically evaluate from their own lived experience, instead of from what they are being told about themselves.

"I came out in college in the Gay Student Union," one guy said. "And I took a queer theory class."

"I see. And in your American history class, did they include AIDS or ACT UP as a fundamental part of U.S. history of the twentieth century?"

"No."

I already knew that the answer was no. Jim and I had gone to the American Historical Association Conference to try to integrate ACT UP into core U.S. history curriculums. But the only people who came to our talk were other queers.

"So, what do you think about that? Is it enough for queer things to be marginalized into one class?"

"It never occurred to me. I didn't think about it."

As we continued to talk, more emerged. The woman's book did not have primary lesbian content. The art world she was situating herself in, excluded lesbian authors whose work did. Instinctively she had figured out that for professional advancement, this was the way to go. To her it was expected, and to me it was closeted. I detected that she felt strangely superior for getting the access one gets by avoiding lesbian content, even though her choices were not making anything better. And yet she was personally out with those people. Just not artistically. There was a contradiction here. How did one part of her life affect the other?

As the conversation continued it was clear that these were divided people. As artists as well as queers, these people wanted to be able to think in radical ways, to have insights, to *realize,* to make work that was outside of social assumptions, to be radical people who could—like the weary ACT UPers—achieve justice in some fashion. They admired their predecessors who had created change through confrontation, alienation, and truth telling. But their professional instincts led them in different directions: accommodation, social positioning, even unconscious maneuvering of the queer content they did have so that it was depoliticized, personalized, and not about power.

A month later I was talking to a young man whom I like very much.

"You know," he said. "I'm interested in making work about an artist who died of AIDS."

"Oh, who?" I asked.

"I don't know yet. I've been looking at people who are unknown."

"Like who?"

"Well, I'm interested in someone named Patrick Angus. And in another one named Mark Morrisroe." He said these two names with a kind of contemporary upslide at the end. Like they were questions: Patrick An*gus?* Mark Morris*roe?*

"Those are both really well known artists," I said, realizing that these two were among many who had not been properly historicized. "Mark Morrisroe has a catalogue raisonné."

"Oh," he said. "Do you know any artists who died of AIDS who no one's ever heard of?"

"There are thousands," I said.

I loved that he wanted to know, and hated that he didn't get it, didn't understand what was missing, how much is gone. How would he?

Another young man, similarly likeable and attractive, asked if he could come over and interview me. When he came to my apartment, I was surprised by the tenor of the interview. There was no urgency. He didn't have—as I expected he would—theories or ideas or passions that he wanted to talk over. I had hoped that he would bring new ideas into my life, but instead he wanted them from me. He didn't have something that he *needed* to know. He just wanted me to give him the interview. Recite my stories. I realized that he was looking for something to care about. He was looking for a hook.

We never discussed if he was HIV-positive, how he negotiated sex, how he had internalized the conflicting message of AIDS.

Ironically, a parallel experience occurred in my classroom at the College of Staten Island. That semester I was teaching night school. I had thirty-five kids of sixteen different nationalities in a *writing workshop*. Most of the kids who attend the College of Staten Island are working class or poor, many are immigrants. I had been at my job for eleven years, but it didn't take more than the first few months for me to learn that Staten Island is hell for queer kids. Year after year my colleague, queer theorist Matt Brim, and I cry on the night bus coming home from work about how profoundly traumatized our queer students are. We do everything we can to intervene but for most of them, by the time they get to us, it's too late. This night a girl, Michelle, came out in class. She had been taking my courses for two years and had never given any sign of being queer, but this one evening she read a story about falling in love with a girl in high school and starting a passionate sexual relationship. When her parents found out, they gave her an ultimatum. If she wanted to have a family, she would have to break up with her girlfriend. Without much thought, she followed their instructions. Three years later, waiting in the bathroom line of a Staten Island straight dive bar, she met another woman and fell in love. In her story, Michelle described uncontrollable desire, accompanied by the knowledge of the tremendous familial punishment that lurked, waiting to pounce. And it did. After one year together, again there was a terrible showdown with her family when they confronted her with her hidden cache of *L Word* DVDs. There was another ultimatum, and finally she again broke up with her lover in order to have parents. At the end of the story, the protagonist finds a boyfriend, Danny. She says that she is able to "be comfortable" with him. And the story closes with her parents gleefully welcoming Danny into their home to watch the football game, offering him a glass of beer.

Later in my office, Michelle tells me, "I know my parents love and support me. This is just too hard for them to understand."

I say nothing, but I know that her parents do not love and do not support her. All they care about are themselves. They do not see her as real. And for now, she agrees with them.

Although the young queer artists and Michelle come from diametrically opposed class positions, they are having a similar experience rooted in a lack of consciousness. For some reason, neither has any cultural context for being able to imagine a more humane, truthful, and open way of life, in which their expressions and self-perceptions would not have to be diminished for the approval of straight people. To be more assertive about their own experience.

After that conversation, Jim and I sat down and reevaluated what we had been doing. All these years of conducting interviews, we had been focused on conveying the heroism of ACT UP. But we had not succeeded at conveying the suffering. We had not conveyed how profoundly oppressed we had been, and how we were able to see clearly and act effectively despite that. And we certainly had not addressed the consequences of AIDS on the living. No one had.

Something had happened between A and B. Something had been erased. Some truth had been forgotten and replaced.

A new arena of thought emerged in my mind. *What happened* was no longer the most pressing question. We had made progress in starting to document what had happened. Anyone could find out by reading the Oral History Project.

Instead, I was being compelled by a much more complex question: What were the consequences of AIDS?

How did it happen that there were two such different trajectories of consequence? That there was the suffering and trauma for some, and the vague unknowingness for others? What was the mechanism that obscured the reality and replaced it with something false, palatable, and benign? Something diminishing and destructive and yet that appeared so neutral? With this paradigm in place, I continued to watch my own experiences.

I was invited to Hartford, Connecticut, one of the poorest cities in the country, to speak to an organization for women with AIDS. The HIV-positive women in the audience were mostly Black and Latina. Like every other person with AIDS in the world, they had become infected through injection drug use or unsafe sex with infected partners. Now they were students, community workers, safe sex educators, peer counselors. Many described themselves to me as "activists," but actually they were working for social service agencies, or as part of AIDS bureaucracies. The distinction between service provision and activism has become elusive. Poor people are very interwoven into state agencies: there's a lot of surveillance and intersection. My life has shown me that activists win policy changes, and bureaucracies implement them. In a period like the present where there is no real activism, there are only bureaucracies. So, when there are severe budget cuts, lack of jobs, lack of educational opportunities, foreclosures, et cetera, there are no structures in place radical enough to be able to mobilize people to respond effectively. These women were under siege by U.S. government policies, but had no political movement, only a social service sector to occupy.

My talk was about the history of the women with AIDS empowerment movement. I read them a piece I had published twenty-three years before in the *Village Voice* about women being excluded from experimental drug trials. The article included quotes from interviews with pharmaceutical executives about how "unreliable" women were, not dependable like "art professionals" (their euphemism for gay men). I then showed a sixteen-minute excerpt from Jim's film, about ACT UP's four-year campaign to change the Center for Disease Control's definition of AIDS so that women could get benefits. The film showed the early leaders of the women with AIDS movement, Black and Latina women—just like those in the audience. Katrina Haslip, Iris De La Cruz, Phyllis Sharpe—ex-prisoners, ex-addicts, ex-prostitutes, now leading a political movement, literally yelling and screaming in the rain in front of government buildings demanding policy changes. Jim had superimposed the birth dates and death dates under the name of each activist, so it quickly became clear that all of these leaders had died.

When the lights came up, there was a kind of stunned silence. Later, I heard from many women in the audience, that they had *no idea* that any of this had ever happened. They did not know that women had ever been excluded from treatment, they did not know that women couldn't get benefits—and most importantly, they did not know that women exactly like themselves had been leaders and activists forcing government agencies to change their policies. Even though they were currently underserved, losing benefits through budget cuts, and in desperate need of an activist movement for poor people in America, they did not know their own legacy of leadership. They did not know that they could change the world, and that people in exactly their circumstance had already done so.

On the way home these images were reeling in my mind. The truth of complexity, empowerment, the agency of the oppressed, *replaced* by an acceptance of banality, a concept of self based falsely in passivity, an inability to realize one's self as a powerful instigator and agent of profound social change.

What is this process? What is this thing that *homogenizes* complexity, difference, dynamic dialogic action for change and *replaces* it with sameness? With a kind of institutionalization of culture? With a lack of demand on the powers that be? With containment?

My answer to that question, always came back to the same concept: gentrification.

First I needed to define my terms. To me, the literal experience of gentrification is a concrete replacement process. Physically it is an urban phenomena: the removal of communities of diverse classes, ethnicities, races, sexualities, languages, and points of view from the central neighborhoods of cities, and their replacement by more homogenized groups. With this comes the destruction of culture and relationship, and this destruction has profound consequences for the future lives of cities.

But in the case of my particular question, while literal gentrification was very important to what I was observing, there was also a spiritual gentrification that was affecting people who did not have rights, who were not represented, who did not have power or even consciousness about the reality of their own condition. There was a gentrification of the mind, an internal replacement that alienated people from the concrete process of social and artistic change.

So I set out to write this book and articulate how

- the unexplored consequences of AIDS
- and the literal gentrification of cities
- created a diminished consciousness about how political and artistic change get made.

A number of interesting obstacles presented themselves as I worked.

1. None of this can be proven. There are no statistics, footnotes or quantitative studies I can cite, conduct, or synthesize which can prove that the consequences of suffering combined with the homogenization of cities produces a change in consciousness.

2. Therefore, it is best to acknowledge from the beginning that this book is really a personal intellectual memoir of what I have observed, experienced, and come to understand. It is not a scholarly or academic book. If I were an academic, I might describe my thesis this way: "A certain urban ecology of queer subcultural existence has been wiped out, through both AIDS and gentrification; this ecocide has resulted in less diversity. The author seeks to address this through radical insights and knowledge of vanished practices and the landscapes that necessitated them" (adopted from an anonymous reader's very helpful report submitted to the University of California Press about this manuscript). The reader also generously commented that the book "comes from a particular subcultural experience and is a valuable account of that subculture, as being a pertinent comment by a member of that subculture on large-scale issues of general importance."

3. That the gentrification of book publishing raises serious formal questions about how this story should be told.

I mean, let's face it. In another era the late, fiercely radical, lesbian visionary Jill Johnston could publish hardcover books in mainstream corporate publishing houses *with no capital letters.*

Now she would have to self-publish *Lesbian Nation*, and no one would know it existed. How ideas are allowed to be expressed has narrowed considerably in the current era.

In the period in which I emerged as a writer, the 1980s, small and large presses published books of queer ideas that were not academic. And even I managed to publish with both Duke University Press and Routledge without a single footnote. But times have changed. The town/gown split which makes the academy the home of much of the new work in queer thinking means that university presses too have become more narrow and professionalized in terms of what kinds of queer work they are willing to present.

I am, after all, an artist who has published a number of books that are highly formally inventive. My novels, *Empathy* (1992) and *The Mere Future* (2009), in particular are not middlebrow literary novels, but rather use associative thinking, collage, wordplay, juxtaposition of materials, and other long-recognized methods of art practice to convey ideas so complex that derivative conventional narrative constructions would not do those ideas justice. In other words, some ideas have to be formally replicated, instead of being described. They have to be evoked. This is especially true when talking about urban experience. What music best evokes life in cities? Improvisational jazz, real rock and roll, and rap/hip-hop/sampling. It's the clash of systems that produces the authentic representation of the complex whole.

Because the idea of *The Gentrification of the Mind* is an abstract one, although based in the realest, most fundamental experiences of being alive, there are places in this book where ideas are expressed cumulatively. They are not just laid out, or told, or recounted, but rather are revealed by the reader's taking in graphs, interviews, affidavits, dispersed anecdotes, profound shifts in place—by letting it all sink in and add up.

This style means that each reader will have a different experience of the book. Which to me, is an antigentrification process: individuation of perception. Or perhaps I'm just an old school avant-guardian, and I don't like things to be formally predictable or bland. I realize that a certain uniformity of standard is inherent in the idea of the academy, but in this case, I rely enormously on the intellectual and aesthetic open-mindedness of the University of California Press, my editor Niels Hooper, and the kind anonymous reader, to allow the book to live and let the public experience and judge for themselves.

But as a reader myself, I have always most enjoyed books that I can be interactive with. I like to fiercely agree with one idea—and fiercely disagree with the next. That kind of dynamic relationship requires a lot of ideas coming at once, from which the reader can pick and choose. Nothing bores me more than the one-long-slow-idea book, and I promise to never write one.

I do not know who will be the president of the United States when you get around to reading this. Will it be some fascist Christian idiot whose supporters don't have the ability to conceptualize? Will it be a pure capitalist who is pro-choice but sells off public hospitals to his real estate developer friends to build even more luxury housing? Will it be Zelig Obama, the man who just wants to be liked, or Super–Franklin Delano–Obama, the guy who brought jobs, housing, health care, equal rights, and education to all Americans? Will gay Afghanis beg gay American soldiers to stop killing them in the name of Queer Nation? Will the market continually crash so that no one who has a job will ever be able to retire and everyone who is unemployed will never work again? Will a two-bedroom apartment with an elevator in Manhattan ever go below $900,000? Will there be a successful multicharacter play by an out lesbian author with an authentically lesbian protagonist in the American repertoire? Will my school not run out of paper and toner by January, so that the teachers won't have to pay for xeroxing out of our own pockets? Will everything (books, music, pornography, education, movies, friendship, camaraderie, love, and television) all be free if they're consumed online and prohibitively expensive to experience in person?

Let me make a prediction:

Gentrification, the historic era of urban replacement, has come to an end.

First of all, I would like to put in a request to historians to periodize gentrification. It should go in this order: the Cold War, Civil Rights, Vietnam, the Women's Revolution, the Disco Years, the Boom, Perestroika, and the Plague. Next is Gentrification and then, the Crash.

I claim that—with the crash of the credit markets, the corporate bailout, institutionalized unemployment, the foreclosure epidemic, and prolonged war as the only way of employing poor people—this process, the influx of white money into mixed neighborhoods as a means of displacing the residents and replacing them with racial, cultural, and class homogeneity, will no longer be in motion. I predict that it will stop for a while.

It is true that the damage from America's Second Gilded Age (see Boom above) has been profound and cannot be undone. And destroyed neighborhoods remain destroyed. And gentrified neighborhoods are not going to return to the people who used to live in them. But the remaining mixed low-income communities of our country, where longtime residents, young people, immigrants, and artists can afford to live and mix as equals are in far less danger of being invaded and neutralized due to the lack of credit. The monster that ate New York is taking a nap.

Today, I pass empty storefronts throughout the city and wonder how long it is going to take for renegade theater companies to start renting out those spaces for weekends or weeks at a time, just to put on a show. I wonder how many more expensive restaurants can make it in the East Village. Maybe they will stop opening them. Landlords *could* potentially care that the only companies who can pay their commercial rents are Dunkin Donuts, banks, and Duane Reade. Might we possibly get some stores that actually sell things that people need? That provide community services? I think it's possible. An independent bookstore just opened on Avenue A while Barnes and Nobles closed on Astor Place. This is fantastic news. Can artists figure out how to show and be seen in the midst of this economic moment? I believe that if they are really creative they can. It's a moment filled with opportunity for people who can think for themselves. There are holes in the cultural fabric, and no one seems to be in tight control. Even the horrifying lack of jobs means that the yuppie road that some were blindly, socially obliged to follow is no longer a realistic option for many who were once invited. This means having to piece together "a living" through an eclectic combination of one's abilities, dreams, relationships, visions, will, and skill. Not a great setup for most, but very enriching for all if enough people can take advantage of the moment to create new paths.

We are living in a fascinating, ungraspable time filled with potential and confusion. We don't actually know what is really going on with our economy: Is it a temporary disaster or a permanent one? We also don't know what is really going on with global relationships and human rights. Is the U.S. government really just a dusty one-room office in the subbasement of global capital? Are alliances and enmities just a performance? Whatever the "reality," no one can say for sure how Americans, or at least Blue State Americans (let's secede from the Reds and get it over with), are going to come to understand this shifting experience of self and other. I do, however, believe that there is more potential for progressive human relationship within the multitude of crisis than there was during the blindly engorged, self-satisfied Gentrification era (the one between the Plague and the Crash). In order to shed its chains we have to at least try to understand. This book is my effort to find awareness about what was lost, what replaced it, and how to move forward to a more authentic and conscious and just way to live.

PART I

Understanding the Past

Someday the AIDS crisis will be over. Remember
that. And when that day comes, when that day has
come and gone, they'll be people alive on this earth—
gay people and straight people, men and women,
black and white—who will hear the story that once
there was a terrible disease in this country and all
over the world, and that a brave group of people stood
up and fought and, in some cases, gave their lives, so
that other people might live and be free.

Vito Russo, "Why We Fight," ACT UP demonstration, Department of Health and Human Services,
Washington DC, October 10, 1988

CHAPTER ONE

The Dynamics of Death
and Replacement

We could argue about which American cities are the most gentrified, but high up on everyone's list would be New York and San Francisco.

The most gentrified neighborhoods of Manhattan? East Village, West Village, Lower Eastside, Harlem, and Chelsea.

The National Research Council's 1993 report on the social impact of AIDS recorded Manhattan's highest rates of infection in Chelsea (1,802 per 100,000), Lower Eastside East Village (1,434 per 100,000), Greenwich Village (1,175 per 100,000), and Harlem (722 per 100,000—clearly underreported). As compared to the Upper Eastside, for example (597 per 100,000).

As soon as the question is posed, one thing, at least, becomes evident. Cities and neighborhoods with high AIDS rates have experienced profound gentrification.

- By 2008, 22 percent of Harlem's new residents were white.
- By 2009, the average household income in Chelsea was $176,312.

· By 2010, the median housing sales price in the West Village was $1,962,500—even with the crash of the credit markets.

· The East Village has one of the lowest foreclosure rates in New York City.

How did this relationship between AIDS and gentrification come to be?

In 1964 the British sociologist Ruth Glass coined the term *gentrification* to denote the influx of middle-class people to cities and neighborhoods, displacing the lower-class worker residents; the example was London and its working-class districts, such as Islington.

Of course, enormous shifts in migration and urban demographics are rarely coincidental or neutral occurrences. Usually people don't want to leave their homes and only do so when forced or highly motivated. The impetus can be political events as well as aggressive policy changes that push one community out while actively attracting another to replace it.

After World War II, the G.I. Bill provided great impetus for urban ethnic whites to move to newly developed moderate income suburbs outside of the city. The bill provided low-interest loans for veterans that made home ownership possible for the first time, and racist housing policies often de facto restricted these benefits to white families. This period, often known as "white flight," recontextualized many white families into privatized suburban lifestyles, with a much higher rate of gender conformity, class conformity, compulsory heterosexuality, racial segregation, and homogenous cultural experience than they had known in the city. Built into this was an increased "fear" of or alienation from urban culture, from multiculturalism, gender nonconformity, and individuated behavior. Innovative aesthetics, diverse food traditions, new innovations in arts and entertainment, new discoveries in music, ease with mixed-race and mixed religious communities, free sexual expression, and political radicalism were often unknown, separate from or considered antithetical to suburban experience. An emphasis on new consumer products, car culture, and home ownership itself formed the foundation of values cementing many communities' ethical systems.

In the 1970s New York City faced bankruptcy. The remaining poor, working-class, and middle-class residents simply did not provide a wide enough tax base to support the city's infrastructure. It was a place of low rents, open neighborhoods, and mixed cultures. City policy began to be developed with the stated goal of attracting wealthier people back to the city in order to be able to pay the municipal bills. However, now in 2011 the city is overflowing with rich people and continues to close hospitals, eliminate bus lines, and fire teachers. So the excuse presented for gentrification forty years ago is revealed by historic reality to have been a lie. We now know that real estate profit was the motive for these policies. Tax breaks were deliberately put in place to attract real estate developers to convert low-income housing into condominiums and luxury rentals to attract high-income tenants. Among those most responsive to the new developments were the children of white flight—those who had grown up in the suburbs, with a nostalgic or sentimental familial attachment to the city: the place where they had gone to visit their grandmother, or to go to the theater, or—as teenagers—to take the commuter train and walk around the Village.

It is not a conspiracy, but simply a tragic example of historic coincidence that in the middle of this process of converting low-income housing into housing for the wealthy, in 1981 to be precise, the AIDS epidemic began.

In my neighborhood, Manhattan's East Village, over the course of the 1980s, real estate conversion was already dramatically underway when the epidemic peaked and large numbers of my neighbors started dying, turning over their apartments *literally* to market rate at an unnatural speed.

As I watched my neighborhood transform, it was quickly apparent that the newly rehabbed units attracted a different kind of person than the ones who had been displaced and freshly died. Instead of Puerto Ricans, Dominicans, Eastern European and Italian immigrants, lesbians, noninstitutionalized artists, gay men, and other sexually adventurous and socially marginalized refugees from uncomprehending backgrounds living on economic margins (in an economy where that was possible), the replacement tenants were much more identified with the social structures necessary to afford newly inflated mortgages and rents. That is to say, they were more likely to be professionalized, to be employed in traditional ways by institutions with economic power and social recognition, to identify with those institutions, to come from wealthier families, and to have more financial support from those families. So the appearance and rapid spread of AIDS and consequential death rates coincidentally enhanced the gentrification process that was already underway.

The process of replacement was so mechanical I could literally sit on my stoop and watch it unfurl.

The replacement tenants had a culture of real privilege that they carried with them. I know that's a word that is bandied about, and can be applied too easily in many arenas. But what I mean in the case of the gentrifiers is that they were "privileged" in that they did not have to be aware of their power or of the ways in which it was constructed. They instead saw their dominance as simultaneously nonexistent and as the natural deserving order. This is the essence of supremacy ideology: the self-deceived pretense that one's power is acquired by being deserved and has no machinery of enforcement. And then, the privileged, who the entire society is constructed to propel, unlearn that those earlier communities ever existed. They replaced the history and experience of their neighborhoods' former residents with a distorted sense of themselves as timeless.

That "those people" lost their homes and died is pretended away, and reality is replaced with a false story in which the gentrifiers have no structure to impose their privilege. They just naturally and neutrally earned and deserved it. And in fact the privilege does not even exist. And, in fact, if you attempt to identify the privilege you are "politically correct" or oppressing them with "reverse racism" or other nonexistent excuses that the powerful invoke to feel weak in order to avoid accountability. Gentrification is a process that hides the apparatus of domination from the dominant themselves.

Spiritually, gentrification is the removal of the dynamic mix that defines urbanity—the familiar interaction of different kinds of people creating ideas together. Urbanity is what makes cities great, because the daily affirmation that people from other experiences are real makes innovative solutions and experiments possible. In this way, cities historically have provided acceptance, opportunity, and a place to create ideas contributing to freedom. Gentrification in the seventies, eighties, and nineties replaced urbanity with suburban values from the sixties, seventies, and eighties, so that the suburban conditioning of racial and class stratification, homogeneity of consumption, mass-produced aesthetics, and familial privatization got resituated into big buildings, attached residences, and apartments. This undermines urbanity and recreates cities as centers of obedience instead of instigators of positive change.

Just as gentrification literally replaces mix with homogeneity, it enforces itself through the repression of diverse expression. This is why we see so much quashing of public life as neighborhoods gentrify. Permits are suddenly required for performing, for demonstrating, for dancing in bars, for playing musical instruments on the street, for selling food, for painting murals, selling art, drinking beer on the stoop, or smoking pot or cigarettes. Evicting four apartments and replacing them with one loft becomes reasonable and then desirable instead of antisocial and cruel. Endless crackdowns on cruising and "public" sex harass citizens. The relaxed nature of neighborhood living becomes threatening, something to be eradicated and controlled.

Since the mirror of gentrification is representation in popular culture, increasingly only the gentrified get their stories told in mass ways. They look in the mirror and think it's a window, believing that corporate support for and inflation of their story is in fact a neutral and accurate picture of the world. If all art, politics, entertainment, relationships, and conversations must maintain that what is constructed and imposed by force is actually natural and neutral, then the gentrified mind is a very fragile parasite.

Eviction of the weak has always been a force in the development of New York City. First Native Americans were removed. In 1811, Manhattan was laid out in a series of grids in order to make real estate sales and development easier to control. Then farmers were displaced. Then African Americans who lived in what is now Central Park. Then working-class and poor neighborhoods were eliminated to build the Brooklyn Bridge. The Depression produced mass evictions. And Robert Moses's highway systems replaced more working-class communities.

Of course, New York relies on new voices and visions. Our soul has always been fed by new arrivals from other countries and from around the United States who enrich and deepen our city. New York has also always been a utopian destination for heartland whites who were ostracized or punished in their conforming hometowns. Individuated young people came to New York to "make it," to come out, to be artists, to make money, to have more sophisticated experiences, to have sex, to escape religion, and to be independent of their families. No one is inherently problematic as a city-dweller because of his/her race or class. It is the ideology with which one lives that creates the consequences of one's actions on others. Many whites over the centuries have come to New York explicitly to discover and live the dynamic value of individuality in sync with community, instead of simply parroting the way their parents and neighbors lived in their place of birth.

As artist Penny Arcade wrote in her 1996 performance piece "New York Values," "bohemia has nothing to do with poverty or with wealth. It is a value system that is not based on materialism. . . . There are people who go to work every day in a suit and tie who are bohemian and will never have a bourgeois mentality like the loads of people who graduate from art school and are completely bourgeois. . . . There is a gentrification that happens to buildings and neighborhoods and there is a gentrification that happens to ideas." The difference between the refusenik Americans of the past, and the ones who created gentrification culture is that in the past young whites came to New York to become New Yorkers. They became citified and adjusted to the differences and dynamics they craved. This new crew, the professionalized children of the suburbs, were different. They came not to join or to blend in or to learn and evolve, but to homogenize. They brought the values of the gated community and a willingness to trade freedom for security. For example, neighborhoods became defined as "good" because they were moving towards homogeneity. Or "safe" because they became dangerous to the original inhabitants. Fearful of other people who did not have the privileges that they enjoyed, gentrifiers—without awareness of what they were doing—sought a comfort in overpowering the natives, rather than becoming them. From Penny Arcade: "I often hear yuppies say that I and other artists were the ones who initially gentrified our neighborhood. But the truth is that we moved into these slums without ever having the need or desire to open a cute café or boutique. We lived among our neighbors as they did."

Serving this domination mentality were new kinds of businesses, ones that opened up only to sell to these newly arrived consumers—something like the hard currency kiosks in the Soviet Union that sold Marlboros to apparatchiks and tourists. A gentrifying business might open on an integrated block, but only the most recently arrived gentry would use it. It had prices, products, and an aesthetic cultural style derived from suburban chain store consumer tastes that were strange and alienating to New Yorkers, many of whom had never seen a chain store. I know that when I grew up there was no fast food in New York City. McDonald's, malls, shopping centers were all mysterious phenomena that belonged to someone else.

These new businesses were more upscale than most chains, but had interior designs that referred to deracinated aesthetics. For example, the foodie thing is in part a rejection of authentic, neighborhood–based ethnic cooking. In the East Village there was the National, a café run by two Cuban lesbians, and the Orchidia, an Ukrainian/Italian place, run by Ukrainians and Italians. Leshko's, Odessa, and Veselka were Ukrainian owned; Veniero's and DiRoberti's served Italian pastries made by their Italian owners. Places to get Dominican rice, beans, chicken, and plantains abounded, all run by Dominicans, and the Second Avenue Deli was owned by Jews. And of course every New Yorker went to Chinatown, Harlem, Little Italy, Arthur Avenue, and the four corners of Brooklyn to eat. Eating food from "other " cultures meant going to businesses where people from those ethnicities were both the bosses and the other customers. It meant loving and appreciating their food on their terms, and happily, at their prices. Gentrification brought the "fusion" phenomena—toned-down flavors, made with higher quality ingredients and at significantly higher prices, usually owned by whites, usually serving whites. It was a replacement cuisine that drove authentic long-standing establishments into bankruptcy and became an obsession for the gentrifiers, serving as a frontline, propelling force of homogenization. The fusion yuppie restaurant would open, and the neighborhood would know it was under siege. The new gentry would then emerge and flock to the comforting familiarity of those businesses, with their segregating prices, while the rest of their neighbors would step around them.

I remember around 1980 when the first art gallery came to East Eleventh Street and Avenue C. They had an opening to which many attendees arrived by limo, reflecting the patrons' fear of the neighborhood and their knowledge that it would be hard to find a taxi at the end of the night. It was the beginning of Loisaida ("Lower Eastside" with a Latino accent) being called "Alphabet City" (Avenues A, B, and C) and turned into a destination location for out-of-neighborhood whites wanting something besides drugs. The gallery owners served oysters and champagne. The residents of the block sat on stoops and watched, stared as the patrons stepped out of their cars in little black dresses, drinking champagne. There was no interaction between the two worlds. I too sat and watched with two lesbian friends, both painters with no relationship to this new gallery scene. Our reactions were benign. No sense of threat. No understanding that this was the wave of the future. At the moment it only seemed absurd, a curiosity. The next thing I remember was a restaurant called Hawaii Five-O opening on Avenue A between a bodega and a Polish pirogi place. It was the first time I was aware of a restaurant being named after a television show. We peeked through the window at the interior, which was a bit like the inside of a refrigerator. I guess that was industrial minimalism. Almost immediately it was filled with a kind of person unfamiliar to us, wearing clothes and paying prices that came from another place. We loved Avenue A because we could be gay there, live cheaply, learn from our neighbors, make art—all with some level of freedom. We did not understand why anybody would want to go to Avenue A and then eat at Hawaii Five-O. But surprisingly there were many people who did want to do this. People we did not know.

That was one of the bizarre things about these new businesses. They would open one day and be immediately packed, as though the yuppies were waiting in holding pens to be transported en masse to new, ugly, expensive places. Quickly the battle was on and being waged block by block until the original tenants had almost nowhere to go to pay the prices they could afford for the food and items they recognized and liked.

So the Orchidia got replaced by a Steve's Ice Cream, and then by a Starbucks. The used refrigerator store and Nino Catarina's Italian wholesale grocery were replaced by a series of expensive restaurants who put whirring motors on the roof of our building and made it impossible to sleep. The corner bodega that sold tamarind, plantain, and yucca was replaced by an upscale deli that sells Fiji Water, the emblematic yuppie product. Habib's falafel stand, where he knew everyone on the block and put extra food on your plate when you were broke—he was replaced by a "Mexican" restaurant run by an NYU MBA who never puts extra food on your plate. An Asian fish store was replaced by an upscale restaurant. The Polish butcher was replaced by a suburban bar. The dry cleaner was replaced by a restaurant. Wilfred, the Dominican tailor, was replaced by a gourmet take-out store. Now if I want to buy fresh meat or fish, I have to go to Whole Foods (known as "Whole Paycheck"), which is ten blocks away. Rents in my building have gone from $205 per month to $2,800 per month. And to add insult to injury, these very square new businesses that were culturally bland, parasitic and very American, coded themselves as "cool" or "hip" when they were the opposite. When they were in fact homogenous, corporate, boring, and destructive of cultural complexity.

There is a weird passivity that accompanies gentrification. I find that in my own building, the "old" tenants who pay lower rents are much more willing to organize for services, to object when there are rodents or no lights in the hallways. We put up signs in the lobby asking the new neighbors to phone the landlord and complain about mice, but the gentrified tenants are almost completely unwilling to make demands for basics. They do not have a culture of protest, even if they are paying $2,800 a month for a tenement walk-up apartment with no closets. It's like a hypnotic identification with authority. Or maybe they think they are only passing through. Or maybe they think they're slumming. But they do not want to ask authority to be accountable. It's not only the city that has changed, but the way its inhabitants conceptualize themselves.

Looking back, when gentrification first started, we really did not understand what was happening. I recall thinking or hearing that these changes were "natural," and "evolution" or "progress." Some people blamed artists, even though artists had lived in this neighborhood for over a hundred and fifty years. The theory behind blaming the artists was a feeling that somehow their long-standing presence had suddenly made the area attractive to bourgeois whites who worked on Wall Street. At the time there was no widespread understanding of how deliberate policies, tax credits, policing strategies, and moratoriums on low-income housing were creating this outcome. In 1988 Manhattan was 47 percent white. By 2009 it was 57 percent white—an unnaturally dramatic transformation over a short period of time. But these statistics don't really tell the story. My anecdotal lived experience tells me that surveys don't tell us what "white" means. There is a difference to the life of a city between low-income marginalized whites moving into integrated neighborhoods to become part of that neighborhood, and a monied dominant-culture white person moving to change a neighborhood. Does "white" mean working-class Italians, new immigrants from Eastern Europe, low-income artists, low-income students, low-income homosexuals who are out of the closet and don't want to be harassed? Or does it mean whites who are speculators, or who come to work in the financial industry, to profit from globalization, or who live on income other than what they earn?

Of course this was far from the first time that specific New York City neighborhoods were deliberately turned. The Bronx was famously burned to the ground for insurance money. In their brilliant 2009 (Drama Desk Award–nominated) theater work *Provenance*, Claudia Rankine and Melonie Joseph show how loyal Bronxites who stuck with their borough through the aftermath of the burnout made reconstruction possible. But now these residents were endangered by new developers ready to snatch the recreated neighborhoods back for resale. In his book *How East New York Became a Ghetto*, Walter Thabit shows how in Brooklyn, from 1960 to 1966, "two hundred real estate firms worked overtime to turn East New York from white to black." In *From Welfare State to Real Estate* by Kim Moody, we can understand how developers used redlining, deprivation of city services, and block busting, and in six years transformed Brownsville/East New York (where my mother was born and raised, from 1930 to 1950) from 80 percent white to 85 percent Black and Puerto Rican, while trashing all the social services, including public education and hospitals. In gentrification the process was being reversed, with financial incentives and social policies designed to replace one kind of human being with another.

CHAPTER TWO

The Gentrification of AIDS

Key to the gentrification mentality is the replacement of complex realities with simplistic ones. Mixed neighborhoods become homogenous. Mixed neighborhoods create public simultaneous thinking, many perspectives converging on the same moment at the same time, in front of each other. Many languages, many cultures, many racial and class experiences take place on the same block, in the same buildings. Homogenous neighborhoods erase this dynamic, and are much more vulnerable to enforcement of conformity.

AIDS, which emerged as gentrification was underway, is an arena where simple answers to complex questions have ruled. "Keep it simple" only works if you are an alcoholic who doesn't want to take another drink. In most other areas of life, complexity is where truth lies. AIDS has been bombarded by simplification since its beginning. *The people who have it don't matter. It's their fault. It's over now.* Easy to blame AIDS on the infected, and much more difficult to take in all of the social, economic, epidemiological, sexual, emotional, and political questions. Even treatments have turned out to be combination medications, not a single pill that just makes AIDS go away.

The relationship of gay men to gentrification is particularly interesting and complex. It is clear to me, although it's rarely stated, that the high rate of deaths from AIDS was one of a number of determining factors in the rapid gentrification of key neighborhoods of Manhattan. From the first years of the epidemic through to the epicenter of the AIDS crisis, people I knew were literally dying daily, weekly, regularly. Sometimes they left their apartments and went back to their hometowns to die because there was no medical support structure and their families would take them. Many, however, were abandoned by their families. Sometimes they were too sick to live alone or to pay their rent and left their apartments to die on friends' couches or in hospital corridors. Many died in their apartments. It was normal to hear that someone we knew had died and that their belongings were thrown out on the street. I remember once seeing the cartons of a lifetime collection of playbills in a dumpster in front of a tenement and I knew that it meant that another gay man had died of AIDS, his belongings dumped in the gutter.

In the early years, people with AIDS had no protections of any kind. Homosexuality itself was still illegal—and sodomy laws would not be repealed until 2003 in the Supreme Court ruling *Lawrence v. Texas*. There was no antidiscrimination legislation, no gay rights bill in New York City, no benefits, no qualifying for insurance or social services. There were no treatments. Particularly gruesome was that surviving partners or roommates were not allowed to inherit leases that had been in the dead person's name. Everett Quinton, the surviving lover of theater genius Charles Ludlum, famously fought eviction after Ludlum's death from the apartment the two of them had shared. ACT UPer Robert Hilferty was evicted from his apartment in the mid-eighties when his lover, Tom—the leaseholder—died of AIDS. And this policy was true in public housing projects as well as in private rentals. So for every leaseholder who died of AIDS, an apartment went to market rate.

While, of course, AIDS devastated a wealthy subculture of gay white males, many of the gay men who died of AIDS in my neighborhood were either from the neighborhood originally, and/or were risk-taking individuals living in oppositional subcultures, creating new ideas about sexuality, art, and social justice. They often paid a high financial price for being out of the closet and community oriented, and for pioneering new art ideas. Indeed, many significant figures in the history of AIDS, like iconic film theorist and West Village resident Vito Russo, died without health insurance. So the apartments they left were often at pregentrification rates, and were then subjected to dramatic increases or privatized.

In my own building, our neighbor in apartment 8, Jon Hetwar, a young dancer, died of AIDS after our tenants' association had won a four-year rent strike that resulted in across-the-board rent reductions. After his death, his apartment went from $305 per month to the market rate of $1,200 per month. This acceleration of the conversion process helped turn the East Village from an interracial enclave of immigrants, artists. and longtime residents to a destination location for wealthy diners and a drinking spot for Midtown and Wall Street businessmen. Avenue A went from the centerpiece of a Puerto Rican and Dominican neighborhood to the New York version of Bourbon Street in less than a decade. I similarly observed the West Village change from a longtime Italian and gay district with an active gay street life into a neighborhood dominated first by wealthy heterosexuals and then by movie stars, as new gay arrivals shifted to other parts of the city. Now you have to be Julianne Moore to live in the West Village. The remaining older gay population is so elite as to have an antagonistic relationship with the young Black and Latino gay men and lesbians and transgendered kids who socialize on the streets and piers of the West Village. Organizations like FIERCE (Fabulous Independent Educated Radicals for Community Empowerment) had to be formed to combat harassment of young gay kids of color by wealthy white West Villagers. Gay life is now expected to take place in private in the West Village, by people who are white, upper-class, and sexually discreet.

Strangely, this relationship between huge death rates in an epidemic caused by governmental and familial neglect, and the material process of gentrification is rarely recognized. Instead gentrification is blamed on gay people and artists who survived, not on those who caused their mass deaths. We all know about white gay men coming into poor ethnic neighborhoods and serving as economic "shock troops," buying and rehabbing properties, bringing in elite businesses and thereby driving out indigenous communities, causing homelessness and cultural erasure.

While the racism of many white gay men and their willingness to displace poor communities in order to create their own enclaves is historical fact, gentrification would not have been possible without tax incentives for luxury developers or without the lack of city-sponsored low-income housing. That the creation of economically independent gay development is seen as the "cause" of gentrification is an illusion. We need to apply simultaneous thinking to have a more truthful understanding of the role of white gay men in gentrification. It is true that like many white people, many white gay men had a colonial attitude towards communities of color. Yet at the same time, it is helpful to think about why white gay men left their neighborhoods and homes to recreate themselves in Black, Latino, Asian, and mixed neighborhoods. It seems clear that heterosexual dominance within every community does not aid and facilitate gay comfort, visibility, and autonomy. The desire to live in or to create gay enclaves was a consequence of oppression experiences. Only gay people who were able to access enough money to separate from their oppressive communities of origin were able to create visible, gay-friendly housing and commerce and achieve political power in a city driven by real estate development. This does not excuse or negate the racism or the consequences of that racism. And these observations in no way negate gays and lesbians of color living successfully and unsuccessfully in Black, Latino, Asian, and mixed neighborhoods. But if all gays could live safely and openly in their communities of origin, and if government policies had been oriented towards protecting poor neighborhoods by rehabbing without displacement, then gentrification by white gay men would have been both unnecessary and impossible.

It is crucial at this point to understand how overt and vulgar the oppression against gay people was at that time. There was not even a basic gay rights antidiscrimination bill in New York until 1986. I remember being on a date with a woman at a restaurant called Kenny's Castaways on Bleecker Street circa 1980. We were kissing at the table and the waitress came over with a distressed expression.

"I don't know how to tell you this, but the manager says that you are going to have to leave."

In the same period (1979–82), I was with a group of lesbians at a Mexican restaurant, Pancho Villa's on pregentrification Broadway and Ninth Street. We were sitting on each other's laps and again were told to leave.

It was perfectly legal to deny public accommodations (restaurants and hotels) to gay people. And these events both took place in Greenwich Village!

It took the disaster of the AIDS crisis for New York queers to win the right to legally kiss in a restaurant unmolested. This helps us understand how the implementation of gentrification policy could have been invisible to the average New Yorker, while the presence of openly gay men rehabbing a building was extremely visible.

Although I have spent thirty years of my life writing about the heroism of gay men, I have also come to understand their particular brand of cowardice. There is a destructive impulse inside many white gay men, where they become cruel or child-like or spineless out of a rage about not having the privileges that straight men of our race take for granted. They have grief about not being able to subjugate everyone else at will. Sometimes this gets expressed in a grandiose yet infantile capitulation to the powers that be—even at the expense of their own community. Professor John Boswell stopped the Center for Lesbian and Gay Studies (CLAGS) from coming to Yale because he insisted that its board be composed entirely of full professors, in an era in which there were no out-of-the-closet lesbian or nonwhite gay full professors in the country. CLAGS refused, and was moved by its founder Martin Duberman to the City University Graduate Center. Boswell died of AIDS, abandoned by the social system he so strongly defended. Or Daryl Yates Rist, who wrote a piece condemning ACT UP in the *Nation,* for being "obsessed" with AIDS, of which he too later died. Media pundit Andrew Sullivan produced one of the lowest moments in AIDS coverage, one we are still paying for, when he claimed in the *New York Times Magazine* on November

10, 1996, that we had reached "the end of AIDS." No lie could be more dear to the dominant culture than that "AIDS is over." For from the moment that the *New York Times* told us that AIDS was over—even though it was and is a phenomenon so broad and vast as to permanently transform the experience of being a person in this world—its consequences no longer needed to be considered.

We still have to work every day to assert the obvious, that in fact, there are two distinctly different kinds of AIDS that are not over.

1. There is AIDS of the past.
2. There is ongoing AIDS.

Neither is over, although they are treated quite differently in the present moment.

Ongoing AIDS is both maintained and addressed by globalization—a sort of worldwide gentrification in which specificity of experience, understanding, and need are glossed over by a homogenizing corporate net, and existing knowledge—about medicine, water, housing, food—existing methods of education, and existing international resources are denied human beings in huge numbers so that a small group of privileged people can enjoy happiness.

Those of us still living who witnessed the early days of the crisis know that had the U.S. government risen to the occasion (as many of our dead begged them to do), there would not be a global epidemic today. As well, we know that the obstacles—lack of clean water, economic underdevelopment, lack of health care, the high price of treatments, et cetera—are maintained by lack of political will above all. The need for our side of the world to live off the other and maintain them in poverty, dependency and underdevelopment, is HIV's best friend. And this divide is as powerful internally to the United States as it is globally.

The confluence of gentrification and ongoing AIDS has been a true spectacle. Marketed as "AIDS in Africa," ongoing international AIDS has inspired a kind of insipid charity mentality in the citizen who expresses her opinions through the products she consumes. Gentrifying chain stores like The Gap, which have replaced many independent businesses while creating homogeneity of dress across regions, have instigated programs where purchasing a particular shirt results in a donation, lower than sales tax, to "AIDS in Africa." Instead of sharing the world's riches, the United States has responded with programs both governmental and corporate that fluctuate in their level of support and fail to address the underlying issues. In her book *Dead Aid*, Zambian economist Dambisa Moyo explains how George W. Bush's AIDS fund delivered twenty cents on the dollar to its intended recipients, a rate typical of most international and domestic AIDS bureaucracies.

Regarding ongoing AIDS at home, the March 15, 2009 *Washington Post* reported that 3 to 4 percent of Washington, DC is HIV infected, a higher rate than many West African countries. While death rates have declined domestically, infection rates are increasing. The failure of U.S. prevention programs to raise their percentage of effectiveness gets addressed with the gentrified cure-all: marketing. Periodically changing subway ad campaigns and alternating slogans abound. Offering young men of color free Metro cards to come to "prevention counseling" doesn't change the fact that they are economically, politically, and representationally pushed aside. But the larger problems—the United State's refusal to destigmatize and integrate gay people on our own terms, treat drug users effectively, support reasonable public education, provide health care, and stop incarcerating Black males—these policies are what keep infection rates high. As long as prevention is the American gay man and straight woman's private problem, it will continue to be a public disaster. The insistence on bootstrap prevention has produced prevention campaigns for "men-who-have-sex-with-men" because we recognize that homophobia is so punitive that calling homosexual sex, *homosexual*, will keep people who are having homosexual sex from the support that they need to avoid HIV infection. We decide to replace truth with falsity, to *gentrify* the truth about sex in order to save lives. Lying becomes constructed as "saving." Telling the truth, that "men-who-have-sex-with-men" are having homosexual sex, is assessed as ineffectual and therefore destructive because the prejudice that creates this environment is considered to be unchangeable. Yet this capitulation to and (therefore) prolongation of homophobia has not shown statistical success in lowering infection rates.

On May 13, 2009, Obama revealed his new AIDS budget, a significant disappointment to activists. He replaced a Bush-era $99 million abstinence-only program with a new $110 million program to combat teen pregnancy, but it had no HIV component. There was zero increase for housing programs for people with AIDS. Most upsetting was Obama's decision to break his campaign promise and maintain the prohibition on federal funding for needle exchange. This followed his earlier removal of new funding for HIV prevention from the economic stimulus package, and the announcement of a new program targeting African Americans that had no funding.

Ongoing AIDS also involves refusing to accept that education and job training that give people an interesting, valued social role are the best prevention against drug abuse. That getting into effective rehab should be as easy as getting into jail. That needle exchange should be as pervasive as liquor stores and—as Linda Villarosa pointed out on the front page of the *New York Times* in 2004—that the incarceration of African American men has created an unpartnerable generation of heterosexual Black women, thereby rendering them more vulnerable to unsafe sex and AIDS infection. Finally, ongoing AIDS means recognizing that people become infected, as Douglas Crimp said about his own sero-conversion after twenty years of AIDS activism, "because I'm human."

In this book, however, I am mostly concerned with past AIDS. I am driven by its enormous, incalculable influence on our entire cultural mindset and the parallel silence about this fact. Do you know what I mean when I refer to "AIDS of the past"?

I am talking about the Plague (the overlapping period between Perestroika and Gentrification.) The years from 1981 to 1996, when there was a mass death experience of young people. Where folks my age watched in horror as our friends, their lovers, cultural heroes, influences, buddies, the people who witnessed our lives as we witnessed theirs, as these folks sickened and died consistently for fifteen years. Have you heard about it?

Amazingly, there is almost no conversation in public about these events or their consequences. Every gay person walking around who lived in New York or San Francisco in the 1980s and early 1990s is a survivor of devastation and carries with them the faces, fading names, and corpses of the otherwise forgotten dead. When you meet a queer New Yorker over the age of forty, this should be your first thought, just as entire male generations were assumed to have fought in World War II or Korea or Vietnam. Our friends died and our world was destroyed because of the neglect of real people who also have names and faces. Whether they were politicians or parents, as people with AIDS literally fought in the streets or hid in corners until they too died or survived, others—their relatives, neighbors, "friends," coworkers, presidents, landlords, and bosses—stood by and did nothing.

81,542 people have died of AIDS in New York City as of August 16, 2008. These people, our friends, are rarely mentioned. Their absence is not computed and the meaning of their loss is not considered.

2,752 people died in New York City on 9/11. These human beings have been highly individuated. The recognition of their loss and suffering is a national ritual, and the consequences of their aborted potential are assessed annually in public. They have been commemorated with memorials, organized international gestures, plaques on many fire and police stations, and a proposed new construction on the site of the World Trade Center, all designed to make their memory permanent. Money has been paid to some of their survivors. Their deaths were avenged with a brutal, bloody, and unjustified war against Iraq that has now caused at least 94,000 civilian deaths and 4,144 military deaths.

The deaths of these 81,542 New Yorkers, who were despised and abandoned, who did not have rights or representation, who died because of the neglect of their government and families, has been ignored. This gaping hole of silence has been filled by the deaths of 2,752 people murdered by outside forces. The disallowed grief of twenty years of AIDS deaths was replaced by ritualized and institutionalized mourning of the acceptable dead. In this way, 9/11 is the gentrification of AIDS. The replacement of deaths that don't matter with deaths that do. It is the centerpiece of supremacy ideology, the idea that one person's life is more important than another's. That one person deserves rights that another does not deserve. That one person deserves representation that the other cannot be allowed to access. That one person's death is negligible if he or she was poor, a person of color, a homosexual living in a state of oppositional sexual disobedience, while another death matters because that person was a trader, cop, or office worker presumed to be performing the job of Capital.

In 1987, ACT UP's affinity group Gran Fury created an installation in the window of the New Museum. It may have been the first work about AIDS in a major art institution. The installation was called Let The Record Show. Employing the politics of accountability at the root of ACT UP's ethos, the show featured photographs of real-life individuals who were causing the deaths of our friends. People like North Carolina senator Jesse Helms. Helms had just said that the government should spend less money on people with AIDS because they got sick as the result of "deliberate, disgusting, revolting conduct." In the background of the installation was a photo of the Nuremburg trials. The implication was that the specific people who caused our friends to die would one day be made accountable. They would be reduced from their undeserved grandeur into wilted hovering little men like Rudolph Hess wasting away in Spandau prison. However in the end, our public enemies, people like Cardinal Ratzinger, who called homosexuality "an intrinsic moral evil," Mayor Ed Koch, President Ronald Reagan, et cetera, all got away with it. No one was ever made accountable. Our friend Sal Licata spent nine days on a gurney in a hallway of a New York City hospital. He never got a hospital room. And then he died. No one has ever had to account for this. When Jesse Helms died, his life was marked benignly. His crimes against humanity were barely mentioned. The names of our friends whom Ronald Reagan murdered are not engraved in a tower of black marble. There has never been a government inquiry into the fifteen years of official neglect that permitted AIDS to become a worldwide disaster.

Where is our permanent memorial?

Not the AIDS quilt, now locked up in storage somewhere, but the government-sponsored invitation to mourn and understand, equal to Maya Lin's memorial to the dead in Vietnam? Where is our wall of white marble with the names of every New Yorker who died of government neglect, and blank tablets with room for more to come, surrounding a white marble fountain spouting water the color of blood? Where is our special prosecutor appointed by the president to investigate fifteen years of U.S. governmental indifference and its product—the global AIDS crisis? This corrupt abandonment of our people is far more destructive than Watergate, Iran-Contra, COINTEL-PRO, and every other government scandal that has resulted in special investigative hearings.

Where is our federal aid to survivors and damaged communities?

Where are the children of people who died of AIDS? There must be hundreds of thousands of them. Most children of murdered parents coalesce into some kind of community, but not these. I fear that the descendants of people who died of AIDS do not fully understand that their parents perished because of governmental and societal neglect. Not because they were gay or used drugs. Where is our Nuremberg trial? Where is our catharsis, our healing? Where is our post-traumatic stress diagnosis? Where is our recovery?

The period I address here is the confluence of the waning of the epicenter of the AIDS crisis and the stabilization of gentrification and gentrified thinking. This is when the radical direct action expression of gay liberation began to be overwhelmed by assimilation—one of the principal consequences of AIDS. But I think that Day One of the triumph of gentrified thought was actually November 10, 1996, the morning when the people who ran the *New York Times* (or "New York Crimes" as Gran Fury called them) decided that of all the lesbian and gay thinkers and activists in this vast nation, of all the LGBT leaders who had bravely built our communities for fifty years . . . the person who should be given a platform was . . . Andrew Sullivan. That he was the man who made them the most comfortable. He was the most "Timesy," as an editor there once told me. So they chose him to say in the "paper of record" (the same paper that ignored the AIDS crisis until ACT UP forced them to acknowledge it) (the same paper that would not mention people's surviving partners in their obituaries) (the same paper that would not print the word *gay*) that we had all come to a time that would be known as "the end of AIDS."

Andrew then went on to become the gay spokesperson of choice for the ruling class for almost fifteen years. This statement, one that every queer person whom I knew in 1996 understood to be wrong, absurd, and stupid—this crazy, diabolical, and poisonous statement—earned Sullivan credibility with the power elite. It allowed him to eclipse the actual queer and AIDS community, their organically evolved leadership, and become the gentrified PWA (person with AIDS)—the gay man with AIDS who would lie and therefore replace all the AIDS activists who were telling the truth. Gentrification had to be in place for someone like him to be put into power. He is a symptom.

Eight months later, in 1997, the Key West Literary Seminar focused on the literature of AIDS. It was a gathering of most of the surviving pioneers of AIDS literature, including Mark Doty, Larry Kramer, Edmund White, Tony Kushner, Dale Peck, and myself. The list of names of the pioneers of AIDS literature who were already dead by 1997 is five times as long as those who lived. At one point during the conference, critic Michael Bronski shared a startling insight from the stage. He said that the rubric "AIDS literature" is itself an expression of homophobia, because without denial, oppression, and indifference, these works would be called "American literature." The cultural apparatus was instructing Americans that those works telling the truth about heterosexual cruelty, gay political rebellion, sexual desire, and righteous anger were not to be recognized. It was a living reenactment of Herbert Marcuse's insight into what he called "repressive tolerance," in which communities become distorted and neutered by the dominant culture's containment of their realities through the noose of "tolerance." The dominant culture doesn't change how it views itself or how it operates, and power imbalances are not transformed. What happens instead is that the oppressed person's expression is overwhelmed by the dominant person's inflationary self-congratulation about how generous they are. The subordinate person learns quickly that they must curb their most expressive instincts in order to be worthy of the benevolence of this containment.

Milan Kundera's masterful novel *The Book of Laughter and Forgetting* engages the ways that pretending away the truth cripples the integrity of both individuals and nations. The very privilege of supremacy—the ability to deny that other people are real—becomes the fatal flaw keeping us from collective integrity as a society. Thus, pretending away the deaths of 540,436 adults and

5,369 children from AIDS in the United States of America (as of 2008) becomes a mammoth action of self-deception, with enormous consequences for our decency. Ignoring AIDS as it was happening, and then pretending that past AIDS has no impact on survivors or perpetrators, allows us to pretend that ongoing AIDS is inevitable, sad, and impossible to change.

There is something inherently stupid about gentrified thinking. It's a dumbing down and smoothing over of what people are actually like. It's a social position rooted in received wisdom, with aesthetics blindly selected from the presorted offerings of marketing and without information or awareness about the structures that create its own delusional sense of infallibility. Gentrified thinking is like the bourgeois version of Christian fundamentalism, a huge, unconscious conspiracy of homogenous patterns with no awareness about its own freakishness. The gentrification mentality is rooted in the belief that obedience to consumer identity over recognition of lived experience is actually normal, neutral, and value free.

It is helpful in this moment to think back to ACT UP's politics of accountability: If someone hurts you, you have the right to respond. Your response is the consequence of their violating action. Pharmaceutical executives, politicians who have pledged to represent and serve the American people, religious leaders who claim moral authority—anyone who interfered with progress for people with AIDS was made to face a consequence for the pain they caused. To do this, ACT UP had to identify what needed to be changed, identify the individuals who were obstructing that change, clearly propose courses of action that were doable and justifiable, and then force the people with power—through the tactic of direct action—to do something different than what they wanted to do. Making people accountable is always in the interest of justice. The dominant, however, hate accountability. Vagueness, lack of delineation of how things work, the idea that people do not have to keep their promises—these tactics always serve the lying, the obstructive, the hypocritical.

I've noticed through my long life that people with vested interest in things staying the way they are regularly insist that both change and accountability are impossible.

"It's never going to change," a wealthy, white, male, MFA-trained playwright told me about the exclusion of women playwrights from the American theater. "And if you try, people will say you are *difficult*."

On the other hand, Audre Lorde—Black, lesbian, mother, warrior, poet—told me, "That you can't fight City Hall, is a rumor being spread by City Hall."

As we become conscious about the gentrified mind, the value of accountability must return to our vocabulary and become our greatest tactic for change. Pretending that AIDS is not happening and never happened, so that we don't have to be accountable, destroys our integrity and therefore our future. Ignoring the reality that our cities cannot produce liberating ideas for the future from a place of homogeneity keeps us from being truthful about our inherent responsibilities to each other. For in the end, all this self-deception and replacing, this prioritizing and marginalizing, this smoothing over and pushing out, all of this profoundly affects how we think. That then creates what we think we feel.

CHAPTER THREE

Realizing That They're Gone

When novelist Kathy Acker died in 1997 at the age of fifty-one, she was poised to become recognized as America's leading experimentalist. Her predecessors William Burroughs and Allen Ginsburg had recently passed away, and it was—in effect—her turn. Shortly after her death, a conference was organized in her honor at New York University by her friends Avital Ronell, Carla Harryman, and Amy Scholder, and some of her works were reissued. But, truthfully, Kathy has quickly fallen off the radar. Her books are rarely taught, and younger writers seem unaware of her huge influence. What I tend to tell my students is that "when you look in the mirror and see a smart, angry girl who wants to be free, you're seeing a paradigm that Kathy helped bring into the realm of the recognizable." Although Kathy died of bad treatment decisions regarding her breast cancer, gentrification and the AIDS crisis were part of the reason that she has disappeared from view. In a sense, her context is gone. Not that she was a gay male icon, but rather that she was a founder and product of an oppositional class of artists, those who spoke back to the system rather than replicating its vanities. That's why her death belongs in this chapter.

Kathy started her career by sending out her early works *The Black Tarantula* and *The Adult Life of Toulouse Lautrec* in chapbook form to key people in the newly evolving avant-garde arts movements of the 1970s. In this way she built a small but culturally influential readership and collaborated with a wide variety of innovative masters from Richard Foreman to the Mekons. She was an articulator of the post-sixties bohemian bad girl. Not a hippie but a kind of art thug. Kathy was the girl who knew she had something to say that mattered, who loved sex and music and refused to be obedient. Later cultural movements like punk girls, riot grrrls, rockers, goths, and even, weirdly, the deadly chick lit, can trace their origins to the territory she pioneered and the devoted followings she inspired in her day, with books like *Don Quixote* (my favorite), *Blood and Guts in High School*, and *Great Expectations.* Typically, though absurdly, she was mocked in her *New York Times* obituary by writer Rick Lyman as a "willfully abrasive novelist" instead of as an autonomous artist with a vision. He also annoyingly turned her into a jester by asserting that "Ms. Acker cut a well-known figure in the East Village scene of the early '80s, favoring leather clothes, spiky hair styles, red lipstick and stiletto heels." A lot of people wore leather in the 1980s and as far as I know, wearing red lipstick is not a distinguishing feature worth mentioning in the obituary of an important artist. But that's how the diminishment process works.

Kathy is emblematic to me of one of the stages of gentrification, the forgetting of pioneering artists and their innovative contributions. The challenge is realizing the meaning behind the fact that they are gone, and how difficult it is to individuate in the AIDS era, when the losses are so numerous and cumulative. As Jim Hubbard and I reviewed footage and still photography for his film *United in Anger: A History of ACT UP*, we repeatedly saw faces that we could no longer attach to names. I had almost forgotten Mark Fotopoulos, until he kept popping up in archival footage. This was the guy who used to stand alone at every demonstration with a sign saying "Living With AIDS 2 Years and 3 Months, no thanks to you Mr. Reagan." Every month he would update the numbers. Three Months, Four Months, Three Years. He's in each demonstration somewhere, in a corner, in a backdrop, standing to the side holding his sign. Then at some point he is no longer there. Only when I start looking for him in the footage do I realize that he has become an apparition. He stops appearing long before I recognize his absence, and only when I understand this fact does it become clear to me that he must have died. Maybe one day he just didn't feel well enough to come out with his sign, and then he stopped coming altogether, and then he died.

The dancer Scott Heron told me that the porn theater on Fourteenth Street and Third Avenue, which is now a CVS drugstore, used to have a loop of AIDS activist videos running in the skanky basement. This may be the same place where the artist David Wojnarowicz met his boyfriend Tom Rauffenbart. David wore a sign on the back of his jacket saying, "When I die, throw my body on the steps of the FDA." When he died, there was a political funeral, and then soon after, ACT UP held the "Ashes Action," in which men and women threw the ashes of their lovers, friends, and fathers onto the lawn of the White House. Anyway, Scottie says that among all the porn loops in the basement booths, there was one clip of Michael Callen, one of the inventors of safe sex, talking about how he was going to beat AIDS, talking about his new book *Surviving AIDS*.

German filmmaker Rosa Von Praunheim brought me and Michael and Robert Hilferty to Germany to try to start ACT

UP. We traveled around trying to get things going, but it was too early in the German crisis. They just didn't believe it was coming. In town after town we heard arguments against safe sex. "Why is it my responsibility if someone else gets infected?" was a very common response. It was quite a performance watching customs agents attempt to understand Michael's gym bag filled with pills. At that time he was into shark cartilage as the treatment of the future, and he also confided to me that dextran sulfate, a failed cancer drug that AIDS activists wanted to have tested at the time, "worked." Michael and Robert and I talked a lot on that trip. It was hard to know what the future would bring to these young men before us: Germany did, eventually get an ACT UP, but only after more people had died. One night Michael told me that for the first few years when he came to New York, every evening after work he would go to the baths. He had a little kit of items he would bring, including clean-up wipes for himself and for his trick. He said that he had three thousand penises up his rectum, but that he was sure he knew exactly the person who infected him. He could remember the man's face and was mad about it. Sadly, by the time Scott Heron saw this footage of him in the basement of this porn theater, Michael had already been dead for a couple of years. In the summer of 2009, Robert Hilferty committed suicide, leaving me the last of the three of us still alive. Neither of them lived to be fifty. Today I am fifty-two.

I first met Robert in 1986 right after his lover Tom had died of AIDS. He made two short films that Jim and I showed in the MIX Festival: Cirque du SIDA, which was an intercutting of Cirque du Soleil and ACT UP. And one was a portrait of the empty apartment Robert was forced to vacate after Tom died. I remember him telling me about Tom's last moments. Robert held his hand, looked into Tom's eyes and said, "I love you, I love you," until Tom was dead. Robert had had a pretty privileged life before AIDS. He'd grown up in Teaneck, gone to Princeton. He was good looking, well trained, and smart. The death of his lover and his eviction from his own home was not the way his life was supposed to have gone.

Robert became very active in ACT UP, and continued to work in film. He was one of the principal organizers of *Stop the Church*, when ACT UP disrupted mass at Saint Patrick's Cathedral. He was one of the only people with the foresight to film inside the church during the demonstration. He edited that footage, along with scenes of ACT UP preparing for the action, into a film also called *Stop the Church*.

It was on a walk with Robert across the Brooklyn Bridge that he confided in me about his plan for the film. A short time before, Jesse Helms had denounced a show at Artists Space, curated by photographer Nan Goldin and called Witness To Our Vanishing, about the AIDS crisis. Helms was furious that some public funds had gone to the space, and particularly singled out work by David Wojnarowicz. Ironically this attack from the Senate floor brought an enormous amount of national and international attention to the show and to the artists in question. In David's case, it enhanced his profile and reputation significantly. Robert, like many other artists, was acutely aware of this process and had devised a plan to tap into this potential source of free publicity. He was sending anonymous postcards to right-wing organizations—one I specifically recall him mentioning was the Catholic League—informing them that *Stop the Church* was going to be shown on PBS. Well, his plan worked. The right-wing groups behaved exactly as he had hoped, protesting the scheduled broadcast, which resulted in the film first being censored and then finally shown with accompanying debate. It brought Robert the attention he craved and he spent the next few years traveling around the world showing the film. Unfortunately it was also a Robert Johnson-esque pact with the devil, because he never completed a work of art again.

In a state of very high anxiety about a head injury he had suffered the previous spring, Robert impulsively decided to commit suicide in July 2009. His boyfriend, Fabio, reported that he was "with Robert through his final moments of life." When I read that, I couldn't help but remembering the image of Robert holding Tom's hand, twenty-three years before. He had recreated his AIDS trauma, the unnecessary death of the young beloved, holding the hand of his grieving partner, saying goodbye. Only now Robert was on the other side. The consequences of AIDS on one person's life are very complicated, but as time passes, they prove irrepressible. Ironically, in 2010 the Catholic League surfaced again to demand that David Wojnarowicz's piece in the National Gallery show Hide/Seek, curated by Jonathan Katz, be censored because of an image of ants crawling over a crucifix. David had been dead for so long, and yet, repulsively, he was still being censored. Still having his reputation enhanced by the notoriety. But Robert Hilferty was pretty much forgotten as an artist.

The present does not resemble the past. We went through a cataclysmic disaster and then we took a break. Instead of constant morbidity there was puking, diarrhea, never-ending adjustments to toxic drug combination, a lot of swallowing, and a certain facsimile of robustness, everyone feeling "great." Back to the gym. The funerals slowed or stopped and the neighborhoods were changed, a new kind of AIDS body modification came into being. No more Kaposi's sarcoma and wasting syndrome on the street—they were replaced by the Crixovan Look: sunken eyes and a pot belly. Guys with HIV could bulk up in a way that the steroid-pure never could. They became larger than that even. Some men got their power back, while most of us could not, did not face what we had really endured. Looking back at the gay dead, locked in their youth, their youth is now locked in the past. Eighties haircuts, ACT UP demonstrations, tentative first novels from defunct presses. Memories fade. Men are increasingly reduced to specific moments played over again and many are moments of dissipation.

John Bernd the dancer and performance artist. Something was wrong with his blood but he didn't know what it was. Something to do with white blood cells. GRID. Gay Related Immune Deficiency. His skin fell apart. He got sick so early in the scheme of things and seem to live on will alone. But was it truly will that made some people live longer than others, or was that a placebo for a weaker strain of virus? ARC. AIDS Related Condition. One day on the subway I offered him a sip of my orange juice. He thought twice and then refused. Who did he think he was protecting, himself or me? I've often wondered. He was one of the founders of the People with AIDS Coalition. He came into the coffee shop where I was working.

"How can I get better if you say I have AIDS?"

I didn't know the answer because it was the wrong question and yet uncontestable. I know there is more there. We were in two shows together, all that backstage banter. I saw his collaboration with Anne Bogart on a version of William Inge's *Picnic* and we had a long, long talk about it. I saw him perform many times with his beloved chair, for which he built a custom carrying case. I remember his final performance with choreographer Jennifer Monson, he was so disoriented he could barely follow her. He waved at me crossing the street. I went to his funeral. There, Meredith Monk sang his favorite of her songs. His mother said, "John very much wanted to live." His sister told a story about the time they had gone camping together as children. John became concerned that spiders would crawl into his sleeping bag. His solution was to surround the bag with stones, and then stand up, clapping and singing "Out, spiders out. Out. Out. Out." This is the world before protease inhibitors, clearly the past. The helpless well watching the ill fade, suffer, and then disappear.

Of course memory is a reflection of the self. I recall the moments that meant the most to me, they are unrepresentative and historically subjective. Massaging Phil Zwickler's feet in the hospital while he explained to his mother that, "that's what we do for the dying." I crossed David Wojnarowicz coming to visit Phil as I was leaving, and later saw him retching with pain on a chair in Estroff's Pharmacy on Second Avenue, waiting for his prescription to be filled. Asotto Saint's family was at his funeral. He was a poet and editor of *The Road Before Us: One Hundred Black Gay Male Poets*. His mother knew all his friends' names. His lover, Jan, died before him, and they'd bought a double funeral plot and engraved a marble headstone with the words "Nuclear Lovers."

"When he received an award from the Black Lesbian and Gay Leadership Forum," said a young Haitian woman with straightened hair and a conservative pink cotton dress, at the podium of his memorial service, "I was so proud of my cousin."

I had never before seen the family of a person who died of AIDS be comprehending enough to make that statement. Usually it was quite the opposite, as when Donald Woods, director of an organization called AIDS Films, died of AIDS and his family had his cause of death listed as "cardiac arrest." Asotto himself had to go to Donald's funeral to stand up and say, "Donald Woods was a proud gay man."

After he died, I received a letter Asotto had prepared for me, delivered by his friend Michelle Karlsberg. He wrote, "Thank you for your support of Black Gay Men." I was amazed at how focused and accepting he was, dying with every detail in place. Bo Houston, the novelist, died angry at me for living and continuing to publish while he knew he would never live to reach his potential. All his books are out of print, despite the imploring title of one, *Remember Me.* I visited Vito Russo at New York University Medical Center, he lay in bed with a Silence = Death button on his striped pajamas. He wanted to know everything that was happening out there in his beloved world. Others couldn't bear to think about what they were missing. When he died, the message on his answering machine said, "This is Vito. I'm sorry I'm not here."

There are two guys in particular whom I think about a lot. The one who was my real friend was a writer named Stan Leventhal. All of his books are out of print now. And the harsh truth is that Stan never really became a great writer. But he wanted to be one. My favorite of his works was a short story in his final book, *Candy Holiday,* where he remembers the last man he knew for sure he could have infected. Stan was kind of a hippie—backpack, relaxed, jean-jacket type. He liked to have a Jack Daniels and a cigarette. He took his AZT with bourbon sometimes. Stan read everything and was the first man I met who actually read lesbian fiction consistently.

He lived in a filthy apartment on Christopher Street overlooking the park. It was packed with books and CDs, his guitar and TV. He'd come to the city from Long Island to be a singer and started out on the folk circuit. He'd broken up with the love of his life right before we made friends, and plunged himself into the creation of Amethyst Press, which was probably responsible for the most interesting collection of gay male writing published post-Stonewall. He published books by Dennis Cooper, the late Bo Houston, the late Steve Abbott, Kevin Killian, Patrick Moore, Mark Ameen—all important, underappreciated artists. He edited a porn magazine, *Torso*, for years, and ran it like a low-rent gay *Playboy*. Beefcake photos and one interesting work of fiction per issue. I even had a story published in *Torso*. Stan had a formula. He'd publish a highly intellectual, formally innovative novel by a gifted writer and then slap a piece of beefcake on the cover so that it would sell. His favorite writer was Guy Davenport, on whom he'd written a comprehensive and adoring monograph.

Near the end of his life, Amethyst got wrested away from Stan in a power play and then the new bosses destroyed and folded it. This depressed him deeply. He was filled with anger. I remember one lunch at a Chinese restaurant when I saw tears splash onto his food, only to look up and discover it was sweat, he had such a high fever but was still running around. His true love died. At my final visit to his apartment, the place stank. The toilet bowl was black. Stan gave me one of his books, *Resuscitation of a Hanged Man* by Denis Johnson, which unfortunately I didn't care for. I was surprised actually, usually we agreed on books.

I saw him in Beekman Hospital right before his death. He was bald and shaking and could barely sit up. That was the first time I met his mother, Pearl, whom I thought of at the time as "uncomprehending," but now I guess was just out of her element and lost.

"There's so much to say," Stan told me. Then he told me something I am not going to repeat here. I stepped out into the hallway as the doctor fiddled with his body and Pearl followed.

"Stanley always wanted a hardcover," Pearl said. Then he was dead. Stan's best friends were Chris Bram and Michelle Karlsberg.

"Should I ask Stanley if he wants to be buried in Florida?" Pearl asked Michelle.

"Stan doesn't give a shit where he's buried," Michelle told her.

Like all the living and the dead, I think I see him everywhere, but it is just new versions, young versions of guys like Stan. Most of us seem to be recreated every fifteen years. I see a twenty-year-old me almost once a month, and a twenty-year-old, forty-year-old, sixty-year-old Stan passes by on the street often enough.

Last week I saw a young queen walking by. Coiffed hair, eye makeup, tight stretch pants, scarves. Maybe nineteen. This was the most endangered type of man in my generation, the kind most likely to die. For years whenever I saw a really nelly queen, I felt frightened for his safety. Being so tough and brave about how they looked on the street showed they were bold about their desires. At one point they seemed to have disappeared, to have been wiped out. But then new ones were created. Do they know their own history? Do they wonder why there are so few sixty-year-old versions of themselves passing by on the sidewalk? What do they want to be when they grow up?

Another man I think about a lot is David Feinberg. He was legendary for being the guy who was so creepy to his friends that when he died they were all mad at him and never got over it. He forgot that people have responsibilities to others until the moment that they are dead. He felt absolved because he was cheated out of life. David's books get more interesting as the years pass. He wasn't sentimental at the time, when a lot of people were, and that made the books seem acerbic and special. Now times have changed and the rest of us who care at all have caught up with the sarcasm, hatred, and resentment by the dying. I mean there were two competing aesthetics at the time: the people who favored candlelight vigils with the release of white balloons, and the kind of PWAs who published a zine called *Diseased Pariah News*. David was so angry it was funny, until it became just pure pain. I think the thing about gay people in that era was that we were not really especially caustic or campy, we just were so far ahead of the regular culture that we got bored very easily, and moved on to the next thing just to keep ourselves interested. Although they are out of print, David's books *Queer and Loathing, Eight-Sixed*, and *Spontaneous Combustion* have become documents of justifiable rage and the guts it took to have it.

There are famous stories about David, famous lines. "You can't wear a red ribbon if you're dead." Or the time he hauled himself out of Saint Vincent's Hospital and wheeled his IV across the street to the ACT UP meeting to tell everyone that we had failed because he was dying. He used to stop people in an elevator and tell them that he had AIDS. He went to a department store, covered in Kaposi's sarcoma lesions and asked for a free makeover. Now, occasionally I see a movie in which a character has "KS" but it looks like the makeup man drew it on the actor with a magic marker. Actually these were flesh-eating sores that started out as splotches, little raspberry dots, and then took over a person's legs and arms and face and devoured them. David went to see Terrance McNally's *Love! Valour! Compassion!* with that same portable IV. As each person died they would pass on their IV stands, shower chairs, bedpans so that others would not have to buy them new again each time. It took so much energy for David to get to the theater that night that he slept through the show. This was his direct action for the day, making the audience see what a person with AIDS looked like in the phase when most just disappeared into their apartments until they died.

I remember when David threw a "dying party" in his Chelsea condo. He invited his closest friends and had us standing around eating and drinking while we watched him, emaciated, lying on the living room couch, dying in front of us. Then he had diarrhea accidentally on the couch and ran screaming to the bathroom. Stan Leventhal was there, very sick. After David shit his pants, Stan left. That's when I realized the cruel nature of David's act. He wanted to force everyone else who had this in his future to stare it down right now. No denial. No mercy. He forgot that we have responsibilities to other people until the moment that we are dead. Or as Jim said, "David didn't realize he wasn't the only one losing something."

I visited him in the hospital, it was like a community center filled with friends of ours dying of AIDS. Sarah Petit, who later died of cancer, was playing chess with the guy in the next room. While I was there, Carrie Fisher called David. He had put out on the grapevine that one of his final wishes was to meet Carrie Fisher, so she called his room. After that he phoned his mother and asked her to send him some cookies. She sent them parcel post. Another time when I was there American Express called. They wanted to report some extraordinary activity on his credit card. Someone was buying pairs of plane tickets to places like Brazil and charging hotel rooms. No, David was busy dying. It was his ex-boyfriend who was ripping him off.

This is a story I heard, so I'm no witness, but after he died his parents decided that they wanted him to have a Jewish funeral. The friends were so shell-shocked by his abusive behavior that they lost all judgment and went along with it, getting a lesbian rabbi. The whole works. But the parents got caught in traffic coming from upstate and were hours late, so the lesbian rabbi had to leave and the house rabbi was called in to take her place. When the family finally arrived, he started the service.

"David was a great . . . athlete."

Oh my God, his friends realized, this was going to complete the nightmare.

"He loved to go to the gym."

These are stories but the pain they contain is immeasurable. The impact of these losses requires a consciousness beyond most human ability. We grow weary, numb, alienated, and then begin to forget, to put it all away just to be able to move on. But even the putting away is an abusive act. The experiencing, the remembering, the hiding, the overcoming—all leave their scars.

These are stories, but the pain they contain is immeasurable. I met novelist John Fox once. He was enraged. I met playwright John Russell once, he was delighted. Robert Hilferty and I visited Iris De La Cruz, a member of PONY (Prostitutes of New York) and author of the column "Iris with the Virus" in the *PWA Newsline.* She was on the ward at NYU, laughing, joking, and barely able to breathe. Then we went upstairs to see Phil Zwickler in co-op care. His care partner was his mother, who was only sixteen when he was born. Essex Hemphill and I both gave keynotes at the first Outwrite: Lesbian and Gay Writers Conference in 1991 in San Francisco, and there I saw Craig Harris, so sick he had to lean on the podium, sweating and shaking, to give his speech. As Jim and I ran the MIX Festival together for seven years, and when I graduated, transferred it to a series of younger curatorial talents, every year our filmmakers would die, their work disappear. I saw a gorgeous Super-8 by Mark Morrisroe, of two drag queens acting out Tennessee Williams's play *Hello from Bertha*, and then he died and I thought it was lost. We tried for years to find it for MIX and then gave up, imagining that the flickery Super-8 original that Ela Troyano and Tessa Hughes-Freeland showed in their New York Film Festival Downtown had burned with Mark's life. For decades I remembered the film and talked about to younger people, wanting it to live somehow. And then, in the spring of 2011, artist Dan Fishback texted me from Artists Space, where he had seen a preserved print—and included the news that the drag queens were played by Taboo and Jack Pierson, while Mark himself was the Dying Swan.

When Matthew Shepard was murdered in Wyoming in 1998, I showed up along with five thousand other queers for his political funeral. It was a transitional crowd. There were guys in suits, a lot of younger people who'd never been in a real demonstration, and a lot of friends from the old ACT UP days. The feeling in the crowd was unusual. It was something I'd never experienced at a demonstration before. No, actually I had seen it once, in a photograph in *Gay Community News* of an ACT UP member, the late Jeff Gates, being arrested. Jeff had been part of the Nicaraguan revolution—getting roughly arrested did not faze him in the least. In the photo, the cop held Jeff's head down flat on the hood of a car. Jeff was looking at the camera with a very certain calm. Like he was waiting for a bus. That's where these demonstrators were at, psychologically. There was an absorbed alienation, a lack of concern, really. We'd seen it all. It was an action of the emotionally experienced. No matter how stupidly the police behaved we all knew exactly what to do. There was a beautifully acquired and deeply nonverbal communication. We just stepped around them, kept going forward, ignored them, their horses, their insipid threats. At one point they thought they had us cornered until we simply stepped out onto vehicle laden Sixth Avenue, and started marching downtown, against traffic, *over* the cars. And I realized that this efficiency, this wisdom and calm unstoppability, was the result of compartmentalized grief. This alienation, this total disregard, this lack of fear, this common understanding, this quiet perseverance, the impossibility of either being stopped or getting upset about anyone trying. Our disappeared friends had taken our fear with them. After all, they knew what we did, who we were. Without them, so much of what we the living have done also goes unremembered. Increasingly, I vaguely recall my dead friends and in those ways I vaguely recall myself.

Rereading Stan's novels was a strange experience. This good man who was a loyal friend, who had impeccable taste in literature, who started a literacy program at the New York Lesbian and Gay Community Center to teach gay people how to read, who has a library named after him, who published some of the most interesting gay male work of our era, this guy could not really write. I feel guilty saying that because I know how much Stan wanted to be a great writer. But on the other hand, one of the paradigms we've created about AIDS is that of the dead genius. Of course, most of the people who died were not geniuses or great. They were just people who did their best or didn't even try at all. Some of them were nasty and lousy, others mediocre. Some knew how to face and deal with problems, others ran away and blamed the people closest to them. Stan was unusual because he gave so much to other people, both personally and in his never-ending contributions to the community.

These actions alone make him exceptional. But, as an artist he had—as one colleague put it—"an ear of lead." Yet, his death and loss is just as horrible, even though he never wrote a great book and possibly never would have.

I'm older now than I was when we were friends and when Stan died. I've suffered more and learned more about people. This makes me appreciate him so much more. Looking over the Guy Davenport monograph, I am impressed all over again. How many writers take the time to praise another living writer? Most people can't, they're too small. Because Stan did not become the kind of writer he wanted to be and yet was able to see and praise beauty in someone else's work, he was an exception. That's what made him such a great reader and publisher. He had that rare maturity not to project. Those of us who are experienced death watchers know that many people die resenting the living. But up until the last time I saw him, Stan appreciated other people. When they were evil, like the guys who destroyed Amethyst Press, he knew it and had appropriate anger. But when people had integrity and depth, he loved his friends. How many others can have that said about them?

The first person I really knew who die of AIDS, died when I was twenty-four. The last person I knew died last year, but actually he had a severe crystal meth problem. But for the first fifteen years, the centerpiece of my young adulthood, I watched many people die and suffer and in the end forgot many of them. And all along it has puzzled me that the AIDS experience is not recognized as an American experience, while for me it is *the* American experience. How can something be equally *the* and equally *not*? Because it belongs to people still considered, even postmortem, to be second-rate and special interest. It has not been integrated into the American identity of which it is a product. AIDS most often appears as a banal subplot point in some yuppie's inconsequential novel, or a morose distortion in a stupid movie. But no true, accurate, complex, deeply felt and accountable engagement with the AIDS crisis has become integrated into the American self-perception. It puts those of us who do know what happened in the awkward position of trying to remember what we used to know in a world that officially knows none of it.

Certainly my outlook on mortality is altered by these experiences. I think about the deaths of my parents quite differently than I would have if I had not become accustomed to seeing so many thirty-year-olds in their coffins and urns. I have expectations every day that others should have basic knowledge about weakness and know how to take care of people, how to maneuver a wheelchair. That there is an unquestionable responsibility to pick up the phone and ask someone how they are doing, even if it makes you feel uncomfortable. I guess this was a lesson for me that feeling comfortable cannot be the determining factor in my actions. I feel resentment towards older people experiencing the deaths of their friends for the first time in their eighties—wondering where they were when we experienced it more times than we can acknowledge. I wonder about the parents and siblings and classmates and colleagues of all our dead friends. What do they say about themselves on this matter at this late date? Occasionally, when writing this book I read sections out loud to various people who happened to be around. I could tell who didn't get it, because all they could do in response was recount the one justifying story of the one person they knew who died of AIDS. They made it be all about them. No one who lived in San Francisco or New York at that time, or even now, should have only one story about AIDS. It's like proof that they didn't do anything. If they could stop making everything be about them, and learn something, they would be asking questions. Not telling some banal anecdote.

Looking back on these events of the past allows me to recapture the feelings of the past. I remember feeling accountable to others and responsible to intervene on their behalf, and I clearly remember others who did not share those feelings and how much destruction they caused by inaction.

Autobiographically, the AIDS experience may be where I came to understand that it is a fundamental of individual integrity to intervene to stop another person from being victimized, even if to do so is uncomfortable or frightening. That the fear and discomfort must be separated from the decision to act. Fear can be acknowledged, but fear cannot be the decisive factor. Fear must be separated from action in order for some reach towards justice to be maintained. I understand that the gentrified mind insists on the opposite, that things are the way they are because it is neutrally and naturally right, and that trying to disrupt that "natural" order is both futile and impolite. But I know from having been an AIDS activist that this cultural message is a lie. In a moral world, the message of AIDS activism would not be exceptional or stigmatized, it would be normal and expected.

Gentrification culture makes it very hard for people to intervene on behalf of others. The Nasdaq value system is and was a brutal one. Being consumed by it and being shut out of it are both deadening and result in distorted thinking about private sectors, economic and emotional. Gentrification culture is rooted in the ideology that people needing help is a "private" matter, that it is nobody's business. Taking their homes is called "cleaning up" the neighborhood. ACT UP was the most recent American social movement to succeed, and it did so because

AIDS activist culture of the 1980s was the opposite of gentrification culture: it held as its organizing principle that seronegative people had a responsibility to intervene, to join their energy with seropositive people's own enormous expenditure of energy so that they could have power over their own fate. Under gentrification our lives became more privatized. That zeitgeist had broad implications, hard to challenge. We had to "act out" in a characterological sense, to stand up to it. Gentrification culture was a twentieth-century, fin de siècle rendition of bourgeois values. It defined truth telling as antisocial instead of as a requirement for decency. The action of making people accountable was decontextualized as inappropriate. When there is no context for justice, freedom-seeking behavior is seen as annoying. Or futile. Or a drag. Or oppressive. And dismissed and dismissed and dismissed and dismissed until that behavior is finally just not seen.

Every historical moment passes. The era of gentrification is hopefully an era of the past, although in this transitional moment we don't know what will replace it. McCarthyism passed, even the Holocaust passed. Outliving the historical moment with your integrity intact is a risky business. I'm glad I witnessed the beauty of ACT UP so that I know it is right and possible to intervene on behalf of others, thereby repositioning one's self towards the acknowledgment that other people are real, even if they have less status and are more endangered.

And all this catalog of loss brings me back to Kathy Acker, who was more special to me than all these guys, as a woman novelist who didn't simply tell the culture what it already believed. Kathy and I were friendly acquaintances. I had a very positive experience of her, I was not her equal, I was much younger and respected her. I did not compete with her and—perhaps as a result—she was very generous to me. As AIDS and gentrification have stripped away the context for her memory, I want to take the time to remember her here.

Our first contact came from her. She reviewed my novel *After Delores* in the *Village Voice* in 1988. There was nothing in it for her, believe me. I had no currency, no connections. I couldn't help her in any way. She just liked my book and she said so—how ungentrified of her. One of the organizing principles of gentrified thinking is to assess everyone based on what they can do for you, and then treat them accordingly. But Kathy was acting from the old school—care about something because it's interesting, has heart, and opens a perceptual door. I had picked up a copy of the *Voice* on my way to the Pitt Street pool, and lay on the concrete rim, lazily turning the pages until I suddenly saw my own name next to hers. I was so unconnected that no one had told me this review was appearing or that it had in fact, already appeared. She wrote, "Formed by emotion, this novel is as personal as any lyric poem." I looked out in the sweltering day, the city was so hot the light blurred everything. And so there was nothing but streaks of bathing suits, the parade of skin tones, and the sounds of neighborhood kids. I dove in the pool and started swimming, and suddenly, as I was propelling myself under the surface, I realized that Kathy Acker had liked my book, and I said out loud under water, "Oh wow."

After that sometimes she would call when she was in New York and I would go over to the Gramercy Hotel, where she liked to stay. I went to her readings and that's how I truly learned to read her work. She read out loud with a timbre and punctuation that were not necessarily obvious on the page. Hearing her made reading her work so much easier. When I came to San Francisco she came to two of my readings and asked engaged, respectful, and helpful questions during the postreading discussions. I went to her house in Cole Valley and looked at her massive library. She would read every book by an author. She had more curiosity that way than most people. She had read every book by Norman Mailer, which I remember really striking me as he was entirely irrelevant to everyone else I knew. She took me to a meal at Duboce Lunch, a groovy place in San Francisco set up by Dennis and Cornelius, the guys who had run the East Village nightclub 8BC back in New York. The other lunch guests were Aline Mayer, Karen Finley, Carolee Schneeman, and photographer Mathew Ralston. Kathy and I went to PS 122 together to see Diamanda Galas perform *Schrei X*. The word reached me that Kathy was dying on someone's couch in San Francisco. I never actually heard the entire story clearly, but my incomplete impression is that she had had breast cancer, had decided on a prophylactic mastectomy, but did not have her nodes done. Went to a faith healer and believed she had been cured. I think she even wrote a text about being cured of cancer. Finally Aline and Mathias Viegener intervened. Mathias became the executor of her estate. It is amazing that someone who fought so hard for her work was so unwilling to die that she did not appoint an executor until the last minute. If she hadn't, her life's work would have reverted to a half-sister she hadn't seen in decades. Aline and Mathias drove Kathy to an experimental clinic in Mexico where she died. Thanks to Amy Scholder, I spoke to Kathy on the phone three days before her death. I asked, "What are you thinking?" And she said, "*Get better, get better, get better.*"

In our handful of rich encounters, Kathy and I talked quite a bit about the *Diary of Anne Frank*. Having been born in New York as a German Jew in 1948, Kathy grew up as many of us did—with this paradigmatic document of the Jewish woman writer as visionary and martyr. To be a German Jew of that generation was to feel entitled and endangered. She was born Karen Alexander, from the kind of family known to New York Jews as "Our Crowd"—her family, the Alexanders, along with the Lehmans, Loebs, Ochs, et cetera were the best educated, wealthiest, and most sophisticated Jews in the world. It was at Brandeis, the Jewish university, that she studied Latin and Greek, found her Jewish husband Robert Acker, dated John Landau (who eventually produced the film *Titanic*), and roomed with Tamar Deisendruck, another offspring of intellectual Jews who later became an acclaimed composer. Kathy came from a tiny ethnic group responsible for originating the most influential theories of the twentieth century: Marxism, psychoanalysis, the theory of relativity, and postmodernism.

What she had in common with the tradition of Benjamin, Arendt, et cetera was what Carla Harryman called "comprehensive knowledge." Kathy was a profound intellectual, able to produce work that incorporated so many different dimensions of thought simultaneously that it eclipsed the capacities of many people. She was able to fully comprehend the cultural product of the dominant culture and of the many margins, and therein lay her problem. For, emotionally, Kathy was average. She had no family. She was an abandoned, traumatized person and did not have a noble emotionality. Artistically and intellectually, however, she was exceptional. Inherent in her supremacy was a certain kind of expectation. A complex one. On one hand, she knew realistically the great value and achievement of her work. She was clear and confident of its merit. Her work was grappling with things that matter, both formally and in terms of content and perspective. There was a discovery in the writing. Her books were objects that young women would take off shelves and put into each other's hands. Life giving. She was highly inventive, not derivative. She was very generous in that her work was emotionally honest and explicit. But because she understood the true value of what she was offering the reader, she expected a broad recognition and gratitude.

The great contradiction in Kathy's life was that she had inherited wealth, and therefore her life was not a consequence of her actions. She could live at a level beyond what money she actually earned. Just for the record, having someone else pay for your education, your home, your equipment, clothing, gym, bar bill, whatever, separates one from the experiences of most people. Regardless of how much they may know better, many people who are not the source of their own financial lives are both infantilized and tyrannical. They seem to believe, on some level, that they deserve this advantage. In Kathy's case, her background and financial cushion gave her a sense of entitlement that was unreasonable.

The problem is that most people are average. This includes people who run universities, publishing companies, and the rewards system in the arts. Most people look at something that is not familiar and think it is wrong. Very few people are able to look at an authentic discovery and be grateful. For that context to exist there has to be a true avant-garde, a large, vibrant community of people willing to think, fuck, love, live, and create oppositionally. Although Acker was an object of mockery or neglect from the establishment because of her singularity, she had a context of people, like young me and my friends, who loved and learned from her. Her death, in the midst of the AIDS crisis, was another elimination of free space, another shrinking of the community of noncorporate thinking. Another victory for the power of homogeneity.

As she wrote in *Don Quixote*: "Even freaks need homes, countries, language, communication. The only characteristic freaks share is our knowledge that we don't fit in. Anywhere. It is for you, freaks my loves, I am writing and it is about you. Since humans enjoy moralizing, over and over again they attack us. Language presupposes community. Therefore without you, nothing I say has any meaning."

PART II

The Consequences of Loss

As crimes pile up, they become invisible.
Bertolt Brecht

CHAPTER FOUR

The Gentrification of Creation

Why do artists move to cities? Because they want to be part of the creation of new ways of thinking. One of the reasons I have always loved being an artist in New York City is that we get to hear some kinds of ideas before they are widely available. We get to invent and hear new approaches as they are rawly, freshly born. And then we get to be part of the development of those ideas through conversations in living rooms, on subways, in the audiences of live presentations, in artists' studios, looking at works in progress, watching rough cuts of films, hearing workshops of plays, and over dinner. By the time the book is written, able to find a publisher, actually printed, possibly distributed, and finally available at the mall, about two to six years have passed. By the time those books are purchased and finally read, two generations of subsequent, newer discoveries have already taken place. But in order for us to gather together for this purpose certain preconditions are required: (1) affordable places for unrecognized practitioners to live, have work space, and find time to make their work; (2) diversity of thought and experience that produces a dynamic mutual exposure to varied points of view; (3) stimulation, unlimited raw material; (4) some kind of pleasure in difference; (5) regular, direct access to great artists and their work.

Under gentrification, what is possible for young artists, hence how they see themselves, is dramatically different. They cannot afford to live or work. They are faced with conformity of aesthetics and values in their neighborhoods. Conventional bourgeois behavior becomes a requirement for surviving socially, developing professionally, and earning a living. By necessity, their goals are altered. Reimagining the world becomes far more difficult, and reflecting back what power brokers and institutional administrators think about themselves feels essential to survival. This is a much more difficult environment in which to imagine one's self as an artist, negotiate the expense of art-making, and—most challenging of all—to be allowed, by the tight fist of the prevailing institutions, to emerge without losing one's soul. There seems to be no other game in town. Right now. I believe, of course, that this can, will, and must change. But that would only be possible with consciousness. And so I want to talk about how gentrification and AIDS have created the loss and replacement of the community-based artist—who responds to people and their aesthetic complexities, instead of to power institutions.

People also move to cities to invent new political movements. Gay liberation, like all explosive visions that transform the world of possibility, required urbanity. It was not born in Scarsdale, Levittown, Syosset, or Great Neck. It required freedom, oppositionality, imagination, rebellion, and interaction with difference. In order for radical queer culture to thrive, there must be diverse, dynamic cities in which we can hide/flaunt/learn/influence—in which there is room for variation and discovery. If people who are not wealthy are going to become artists and revolutionaries, they need affordable rents and workspaces, ways to learn their craft without paying tuitions, and a process of development that is not systematized. They need ways of being seen and helped by those in power behind the scenes, without having to be professionalized facsimiles to get help. Most importantly, real artists—people who invent instead of replicate—need counterculture as a playing field.

Most plays that get produced these days are kind of like live-TV. If they involve complex social dynamics, they usually argue, in the end, that people are resilient and good prevails after all. But most often, rewarded plays involve the small concerns of recognizable bourgeois types, and may have some formal innovation for their own sake. I've experienced two talented theater directors telling me explicitly that they don't care about what a play is saying or what happens in a play, they are only interested in how it says it. But formal invention is not inherently progressive, as we have learned from video clips, computer graphics, and sampling. Formal invention has a radical purpose when used to convey unconventional points of view, that is to say when it is used to expand what is conveyed about human experience. Even though many heterosexuals avoid the fate/destiny of romance/marriage/parenthood, it is a well worn and instantly recognizable structure upon which most mainstream representations are based. In other words, most bourgeois straight people already know the storyline their lives are supposed to follow before their lives are even begun. For preassimilation queers, this was not the case. Our lives were strangely structured singular works without predetermination, unknown stories that had never before been heard. The dominant culture told us we were outcasts and alone and then did everything they could to make that come true. Out of the conflict between our determination to truly exist fully as ourselves, and our clash with highly propagandized false stories and even more powerful silences, came queer culture, the marvel that produced many of the great art ideas of the twentieth century.

The artful AIDS dead, of course, included some very successful and high-earning celebrity artists like Keith Haring and Robert Mapplethorpe. But the vast majority were rank-and-file artists who didn't live long enough to become known, or to quit, or to become teachers or heads of institutions. They didn't live long enough to influence. I could list names like Gordon Kurti, Brian Taylor, John Sex, Huck Snyder, Paul Walker, Paul Walker (there were two of them), Harry Whitaker Shepard, and on and on forever. But what would be the point? Since many of them worked before video was a regular part of life, there is little documentation of what they did. In a sense they only live on in the memories of the living. Penny Arcade's brilliant play *Invitation to the End of the World* featured a heartbreaking scene in which Penny imagines the mother of Rita Redd, a drag artist who died of AIDS, standing on a street corner in the East Village stopping passersby and asking if they'd ever heard of her son.

"He did shows!" she insists. "He put on lots of shows."

She can't understand why none of the recent yuppie arrivals know who he was. She doesn't realize that his audience has also died.

These dead and their friends pioneered new art ideas including performance, installation, the intersection of new technologies and live performance, improvisational new music and improvisational dance, drag, expansions of materials and techniques. They came to New York or grew up in New York and lived in low-income areas, hustled legally and illegally for a living, made art for low-income audiences, and had an interactive relationship with urban life. They did not live long enough to be able to object to the professionalization of the arts, which might not have been so thorough had they lived. They did not mature. When they died, their practice of creating new paradigms outside of institutional structures was removed from sight.

A recent issue of the *New Yorker* included a short profile of John Kelly, one of the survivors of the lost generation of radical gay male artists. The author was talking to him about his many years of performing the works of Joni Mitchell, and at one point she asked John why he "did not want" to be part of a recent Joni Mitchell tribute album. "I wasn't invited," John replied. It was such an amazing moment. The *New Yorker* reporter, who by definition has power and access, projected that this important senior artist would have the same. She assumed that he had "made it." And that the only reason he was not being included would be because of his own refusal. She projected power onto this gay experimental artist that he cannot possibly have because of his cultural position. I would have understood from the first second that of course he was excluded, that inclusion in the Joni Mitchell tribute album was not based on talent, understanding, merit, or having something to say. But this reporter, believing that things are different than they actually are, believed that he was now normal.

About a week later I had a Facebook conversation with a reporter from *New York Magazine*. She said she had "read somewhere" that I argued that gay people should have nothing to do with their homophobic families. I informed her that my belief was, in fact, the opposite of that. I told her that my book on familial homophobia argued that third parties should intervene and create consequences for homophobic families so that they could not get away with marginalizing and shunning their gay family members. Again, she skewed reality to create a false but comfortable illusion in which it is the gay person who has the power and who refuses to participate, when the truth is that we are the ones who are excluded.

In light of this contemporary redrawing of reality, I want to try to show what it is like to be a queer artist of the disappeared generation, what kinds of emblematic experiences are at play, and how our values have been formed. So, let me try to piece together that process by looking at some of my favorite survivors. First I want to introduce you to Jack and Peter. And then let you in on a bit of my conversation with Jim.

Jack Waters and Peter Cramer met on stage in the 1970s and have shared the spotlight ever since. The history of their love and work crosses paths with the most marginal and occasionally the mainstream. They move in and out. It's a history of cheekiness, haphazard decision making, and incredible risk-taking. Long-term AIDS survivors, they live in a squat on the Lower Eastside that they have shared for decades with Kembra Phfaler (of the cult band The Voluptuous Horror of Karen Black) and filmmaker Carl George, plus a never-ending assortment of homeless and/or wandering gay kids needing a place to be an artist for a little while.

Peter was a straight white ballerina, performing in *Giselle* and *The Nutcracker.* Jack was a gay Black modern dancer in the tradition of Martha Graham and Doris Humphrey. They met while performing in a middlebrow dance company for Wall Street white-collar workers needing entertainment on their lunch hour. A friend begged them to never do bland work like that again, and so, newly in love, they fled the mainstream dance world forever.

Peter had been a club kid in the seventies, working at the No Name Club (run by Eric Goode and Sean Houseman), a renegade place, constantly shifting its location. He also worked at the A Salon with Charlotte Moorman (an iconic sixties pioneer of the Fluxus movement, collaborator of Nam June Paik, and notoriously arrested on a decency charge for playing the cello without concealing her breasts) and Michael Keane, part of a group called Des Refusees. They worked in an interdisciplinary voice crossing between visual art, ballet, butoh, and performance in nightspots where "club" and "art" were synonymous.

"Neither of us had ever been very interested in the authoritarian way of art-making," Jack said. "We're very social." And so were the times.

Both men were heavily influenced by the historic Times Square Show in 1980, put on by Co-Lab (Collaborative Projects), a nonprofit collective of artists including Kiki Smith, her late sister Bebe (who died of AIDS), and David Hammonds, producing work in divergent places in response to the dead world of blue-chip art galleries, still selling pop art and abstract expressionists. This pioneering show, which is widely seen as emblematic of the new era, was set in abandoned buildings in a Midtown Manhattan that was full of abandoned buildings, as New York City had almost defaulted into bankruptcy. Real estate then was undesirable, so artists had shells of buildings in the Times Square area in which to do their work. Co-Lab was not looking at their art as product but rather for social impact. There were no labels or tags, no commercial intent. In many ways this show was a model for Peter and Jack's sense of what an artistic community could be and do.

With the late Brian Taylor, who died of AIDS, they established a collective called Pool that became the resident company of the Pyramid Club, a drag/performance club on Avenue A where I had my first play, at 2 a.m. in 1979.

"There was a lot happening at the same time," Jack says. "And that was our steady paying gig. Forty dollars a night and drinks to your heart's content."

Fellow Pyramid performers, many of whom died of AIDS, included the late John Sex, the late Ethyl Eichelberger, John Jeshrun (with his legendary *Chang In A Void Moon*—a performance serial), John Kelly, the late Frank Maya, the late John Bernd, the late Huck Snyder, and of course drag queens galore like Tanya Ransom, the late Rita Redd, and the late Bobby Bradley, "this really cute pervert Mormon." The late Anne Craig was the emcee. In the early eighties the Pyramid was a few blocks down from Ela Troyano and Uzi Parnes's illegal Chandelier Club, where the windows were blacked out to keep the fire department from noticing, Dennis and Cornelius's 8BC Club, and Club 57, where Anne Magnuson performed. But the gentrifiers were coming.

"As the Pyramid became more successful, the bridge and tunnel crowd started showing up," Jack says. "So, then we got our own place."

"Bridge and tunnel" was New York–speak for tourists from New Jersey and the suburbs. Later, when rich Europeans started flocking to the East Village and were quickly followed by a bevy of four-dollar cappuccino places, it got amended to "B&T&A" ("bridge and tunnel and airplane").

Some Co-Lab artists like Bobby Gee, Alan More, and Rebecca Howland had established a gallery space in an abandoned building on Rivington Street called ABC No Rio (derived from the half effaced sign of the previous tenant, a Spanish-speaking *Notorio*) and were looking for new directors to take on operating responsibilities. By this time the boys had hooked up with their collaborators: Carl George, the late Gordon Kurti, Brad Taylor and his brother the late Brian Taylor, Edgar Oliver, and Erotic Psyche (Aline Mare and Bradley Eros), so they had an extended community of artists to work with. Jack and Peter moved into the basement at No Rio and a new art energy was born.

For the next four years they ran ABC No Rio with a dizzying revolving door of visual arts, music, and performance. Literally thousands of artists moved through. Then Mathew Courtney started the influential open mike at No Rio, the precursor to the spoken word/slam scene later to come to fruition at the Nuyorican Poets Café. They also housed Amica Bunker, a seminal music series founded in 1984 by Chris Cochrane and Cinny Cole, with pioneer artists like John Zorn, Zeena Parkins, Shelley Hirsch, and Christian Marclay.

"It wasn't a *space,* it was a *place,*" Jack says. "Everyone from Michelle Shocked to Keith Haring to Nick Zedd and Lydia Lunch. It wasn't *curated.* People could just come and draw if they wanted to. It was available. It was there."

One of the aesthetic shifts Jack noticed that came with gentrification was the sudden popularity of solo performance, a kind of alternative stand-up. "To us," he said, "that was too normal." The elaborate epic ritual pieces that Ping Chong or Meredith Monk or Erotic Psyche would do were replaced by a single person standing in front of a mike. This was, of course, the influence of television—instead of inventing forms from outside of corporate culture, the newly arriving crew of professionalized artists were using forms from *The Tonight Show.* Stand-up and solo were a much more commodifiable form to work in. Later, solo performance became the curateable, acceptable expression for minority voices in mainstream theaters, as multi-character *plays* with gravitas, or elaborate works with large casts, remained the arena of the white male. Lesbians, Latinos, and experimentalists were marginalized into the vaudeville solo niche.

Another sign of gentrification was the opening of what was called "performance clubs" like Area in 1985.

"We thought *it's a new club, we're all going to get work there*," Jack remembers. "But when Area opened it was about *display*. It was heralded as a *performance club*, but they put artists into display cases to be looked at as background, not to be heard."

Thinking about this insight, I can see that this was the shift from a neighborhood focused on artistic production into a destination neighborhood for tourists who wished to drink and socialize surrounded by artists as the background scenery. Their primary task was the reproduction of status through sexual, social, and business networking. The class interest came first, and art was its Muzak.

"Looking back," Jack says, "at Area there was less and less interruption of the beat. The beat couldn't stop for performance because the beat was hypnotic and the beat makes you drink and the beat makes you want to stay. If you did a performance that people didn't like and they would boo or walk out, they didn't drink. When the emphasis is on the bottom line, you don't want anyone to walk out."

Here we see a really pivotal moment of change, when art must become something that does not make people uncomfortable, so that they will spend money. The kind of person who is expected to consume art is transformed in the mind of the producer. The people who might very possibly love being expanded by what they see are never given the chance. They're trained to be narcissistic and unimaginative, even if they could be productive creative thinkers. Drawing a connection between the art they see and the world in which they live becomes less available. The long-term effect of such a condition is that gatekeepers (producers/agents/publishers/editors/programmers/critics, etc.) become narrower and narrower in terms of what they are willing to present, living in a state of projected fear of ever presenting anything that could make someone uncomfortable. There is a dialogic relationship with the culture—when consumers learn that uncomfortable = bad instead of expansive, they develop an equation of passivity with the art-going experience. In the end, the definition of what is "good" becomes what does not challenge, and the entire endeavor of art-making is undermined. Profit-making institutions then become committed to producing what the Disney-funded design programs call "Imagineers," the craftsman version of Mouseketeers, workers trained to churn out acceptable product, while thinking of themselves as "artists."

In 1997, I was assigned by the *New York Times* Arts and Leisure section to do a piece on the new theater scene springing up below Houston, centered on Ludlow Street. For thirty days and nights I went to see plays and performances and slowly tried to piece together what this new wave's aesthetic and social concerns seemed to be. At that point, I did not fully understand the new phenomenon of replacement artists from professionalization programs, and was kind of shocked to hear the sorts of things the new theater artists were saying and doing. When I realized, and articulated in the article some of the values this new movement stood for, the piece was killed. But what I only came to understand years later when preparing this volume, is that the new artists had no awareness at all of the existence of the dead people who had lived and worked—just a few years before—on the very streets where they were now working and paying high rents.

"Theater is the new rock and roll for a new audience," Ludlow Street's undisputed impresario, Aaron Beall, told me in 1997. "People who just got out of college want a theater that is fast and funny at the pace at which they live their lives." An energetic optimist, he pioneered the Ludlow Street scene by opening Theater Nada in a basement in 1988. Then he started up House of Candles around the corner on Stanton, the Piano Store down the block, and the Pink Pony Café Theater across the street. The year he and I sat down to talk, he inaugurated the first annual Fringe Festival, which has since gone on to become a huge phenomenon, whether offering out-of-town companies their "New York debut" or serving as a platform for fundraising for the Broadway musical *Urinetown*.

David Cote, who is now a theater critic for *Time Out New York*, and television's *On Stage*, at that time edited *OFF*, a monthly newspaper devoted to alternative theater. "The majority of young directors, downtown, are right out of school," he said in 1997. "Anne Bogart in particular has a lot of influence because she's taught at Columbia and NYU."

In this new scene, the formal concerns of the erased generation were no longer relevant. Some young artists vehemently insisted to me that they were not interested in theatrical innovation. "Formal invention has reached a level of exhaustion," said Trav SD, artistic director of Mountebanks Theater. According to Beall, more important than innovation was "the desire to participate in the theatrical experience. It's fun, deep in a pop sensibility of monsters and robots, Nintendo and Gameboy." And in fact, consistent theatergoing revealed little new formal territory—either, as Beall noted, using ideas from television, consumer goods, and marketing, or very frequent quoting of the avant-garde masters, in a way that rendered their discoveries status quo. Integrated video monitors and the use of handheld mikes in the style of the Wooster Group, choreographed musical sequences influenced by Bogart, and especially pithy one-liners delivered in Richard Foreman's performance style abounded. "Everyone," said Beall, "is derivative of him rather than creating their own theatrical environment, which he did for so long."

While I did hear some pro- and anti-Mayor Giuliani routines at various stand-up open mikes, generally younger companies told me that they hesitated to be politically engaged.

"Issues are for television," said Jocelyn Cramer of the Ground Floor Theater Company in residence at the Clemente Soto Velez Center on Rivington. "We don't want to do disease-of-the-week."

"People come to the theater to be entertained," added her colleague Matt England. "If you make being political a priority, you might find that people won't come back."

"Many artists today don't have to suffer like they did in the fifties," said Montebanks' Robert Pinnock. "They have enough intelligence to avoid it."

Despite an unwillingness to take on social issues, real estate was a major factor in the lives of these artists. Beall's annual rent payments for his spaces came to one hundred thousand dollars. But company members often took responsibility to keep prices low. At Collective Unconscious, a black box theater on Ludlow, the monthly rent of $2,100 was paid out of the members' pockets, filled by full-time jobs at such serious places as CNN.

There were still two Latino theaters in the neighborhood, which was still heavily Dominican by the end of the 1990s. The Milagro was a naturalistic political theater with a focus on neighborhood life, such as Ed Vega's drama *Spanish*

Roulette, about a Puerto Rican poet living on the Lower Eastside, performed in Spanish and English. Company member Carlos Espina told me that the newly arrived white residents received a higher level of city services than their displaced Latino predecessors including "picked up trash, fixed sidewalks, and better streetlights."

"It's ironically sad," said company member Martha Garcia. "We would be happier if there was more affinity with the new theater groups coming in."

Over and over it struck me how straight the late nineties scene was compared to the eighties. There was a kind of Deadwood feeling, a distinct absence of young queer energy. After all, an entire generation of us had died, while straights had continued to live. What was happening with the new generation of queers seemed to be in the clubs, solo performers behind mikes. Justin Bond was the reigning queen of the East Village late nightclub scene in his persona of Kiki, an ageing cabaret singer who squandered her fortune on Canadian Club Whiskey, touring the country with her broken down accompanist Herb. Bond's Marianne Faithfullesque persona was packing the Flamingo East on Sunday nights. Also evolving at that time was the early stage of the drag king scene, which also happened on Sunday nights, at Club Casanova at Velvet on Avenue A where a young, shy, Haitian woman, Mildred Gerestant, emerged as Dred, the drag king version of a macho blaxploitation antihero. But there was no interaction between the straight theater companies below Houston and the late-night queer cabarets above. They simply coexisted in ignorance, only one knowing clearly what it had and what it had lost.

In this scramble period, those who were to live had to restart living. And for artists of the AIDS generation, that meant finding a way to represent their own disappeared context, without being locked in nostalgia. My collaborator of twenty-six years, Jim Hubbard, was one of the artists who took on this burden and responsibility, artistically.

On November 10, 1977, at the sixty-fourth birthday party of gay experimental filmmaker James Broughton, Jim met his lover Roger Jacoby, who died of AIDS in 1985. Jim also got blown that night by Curt McDowell (maker of the great gay classic *Loads*, who also died of AIDS) and he met Roger's other lover, Ondine, the Warhol superstar of *Chelsea Girls*. So, it was a big moment in his life, and in the future of gay experimental cinema. Roger was a transitional figure in the history of gay experimental film, bridging from makers who preceded gay liberation, like Kenneth Anger, Broughton, Warhol, George Kuchar, Gregory Markopoulous, and others, to younger makers like Jim and Jerry Tartaglia, whose entire worldview was forged by gay liberation. Roger's work, to a large extent, satirized and criticized heterosexuality, but did not at first deal openly with homosexuality. He was influenced by Ondine and his work was highly operatic, owing a great deal to Maria Callas.

Roger was a master of a procedure known as "hand processing"—in which filmmakers develop their own 16 mm and Super-8 film, using chemical balances to control color and contrast in the final product. With the advent of digital, video, and computer graphics, this technique has disappeared along with Super-8 film itself.

"He taught me," Jim says, "what it meant to be a filmmaker, to devote one's life to a medium and to self-expression. In retrospect, I don't know how good a model it was. It was a life filled with uncertainty and lack of security, but it was a model that produced great work, expressive of itself in every frame, without *decorative elements,* as Roger would say. That is, without unnecessary moments."

Four years after Roger's death, Jim made his most important experimental film, *Elegy in the Streets,* completed in 1989. It was his attempt to articulate a notion that every person who came to an ACT UP demonstration did so for a personal reason. Either they were HIV-positive and fighting for their lives, or they had someone close to them—a friend, a lover, a brother—who had died. "Roger was that person for me. He was the first person I was really close to who died.

"I'm not sure when I decided to make a film about AIDS," Jim told me. "But certainly by August 1984 when Roger was diagnosed, I already had. I first started filming a guy named Billy, a PWA I met around the time of Roger's diagnosis. He did not like me hanging around with my camera and the filming did not go well. He was a gardener and I filmed his garden." When Roger died, Jim inherited his outtakes. At the time of Roger's death, Jim felt that Roger's work was very different from his own. He could instantly tell which footage Roger had shot and which he had shot himself. But after all those years, it started to feel blended. And he decided to use Roger's footage in his own work.

Jim was the first film artist to systematically chronicle gay and lesbian street rebellions, including demonstrations against the making of the movie *Cruising* and protests following a police raid on a Black gay bar called *Blues.* Often, he'd be the only person on site with a camera. So, it was inevitable that when AIDS activism happened, it would come into his work as it came onto the scene he was already documenting. ACT UP demonstrations included in *Elegy in the Streets* are the Second Wall Street Action (March 1988), Gay Pride (1987 and 1988), Target City Hall

(March 1989), another Wall Street demo, Seize Control of the FDA (October 1988), the Shea Stadium Action (May 1988).

Sometime in 1988, he started editing. There were no appropriate structures available from the formulas of narrative filmmaking, so he looked to literature, specifically poetry, and started reading a lot of pastoral elegies—a form first developed in the second and third century—especially Milton's "Lycidas." *Elegy in the Streets* translates the elements of classical elegy to film. It is silent, forcing the viewer to really look at what there is to see, and not rely on music to convey the emotion. Among the elements he took from the pastoral elegy were the catalog of flowers (symbols of beauty and the brevity of life). The lilacs are a reference to Whitman's "When Lilacs Last in the Dooryard Bloom'd." There is a pan of the vine growing on a tenement where Billy had his garden. Certainly this is an evocation of life abiding in the cruelest of environments. There is a procession of mourners, a visit to the underworld (shot by Roger Jacoby) which features negative footage of the gay street icon Rollerina (Charles Stanley) as the archangel mourning or praying over the body, as in Milton's "Look homeward angel now." And finally the film ends with ACT UP's action at Shea Stadium and "those wonderful kids who are a symbol of hope and renewal." Again, Milton's "tomorrow to fresh woods, and pastures new."

Elegy in the Streets is a film about memory, and the images of Roger usually occur when triggered by an image in a demonstration: when someone looks like him, or the eyes in the Reagan poster evoke Roger's eyes in footage shown in negative. A couple of times he comes out of nowhere, like a memory that suddenly hits you for no reason. Jim tries to present Roger's range of interests—piano playing and filming. But there is no footage of his anger.

Today Jack Waters, Peter Cramer, and Jim Hubbard are still carrying on the old-school values of building arts communities that are open, intergenerational, and not based on caste. Jim is still in the leadership of the MIX Festival, now in its twenty-fourth year, which continues to show new and emerging artists, including those who were not yet born when MIX started. Current artistic director Stephen Kent Jusick continues the vision that, rather than fostering elite columns of producers of passive entertainment, instead art collectives and institutions can actively *create* queer artists by presenting queer work, maintaining venues, and staying grassroots. The goal of the organization is to get the work to marginalized people so that they can imagine themselves making art. And history has shown that open door, welcoming, community-based policies produce both high profile and under-the-radar artists. Not only have many well-known successful makers come out of MIX, but the inclusivity has also resulted in the early development of young curators of color like Shari Frilot of Sundance and Rejendra Roy, now film/video curator at the Museum of Modern Art. Both started as grassroots curators at MIX and have grown to be influential leaders with the knowledge and values of inclusion that come only when one is developed in the community.

Jack and Peter now devote a great deal of their time to Peter's Le Petit Versailles, a squatted community garden, which for the last fifteen years has offered a venue to emerging and senior marginalized artists from the neighborhood and the world. In the summer months there are events almost every night, from films projected onto the side of their building to a wide and wild array of performance. Jack, Peter, and Jim have maintained the old-school value of respecting and welcoming artists, taking them seriously, regardless of their point of view or social position. Today they are, in a sense, living museums of values of the past, but their personal efforts still allow new artists to be heard and seen and to develop. What kind of world the new artists develop into, is sadly, out of our hands.

. . .

> The avant-garde is in opposition to academia. As soon as something is embraced by academia it is no longer avant-garde. If you do not have a functioning criminal class in the art world then you have academia, and while academia is a reflection of the art world, it is not the art world, it is academia and academia will never be the art world. (Penny Arcade, 1995)

> The creator of the new composition in the arts is an outlaw. (Gertrude Stein, 1926)

About ten years ago, I invited a friend over for dinner. I won't say his name because I want to protect him. We had been in ACT UP together and now, he too, was a working playwright. I was amazed, probably "dazzled" would be a better word, at the cruelty, lying, mediocrity, and horrific antiart values of the American theater. I, who had lived through many different art forms and art scenes, had never seen anything so vicious and redundant in my life. How could people who understood themselves to be artists be so uninterested in what is true, be so mean, and so committed to the most banal rehashes of the worst of yuppie entertainment? This was especially bewildering to me considering the potential recognition of human frailty inherent in an art form that is performed live in front of other living mortals.

"It has to do with hierarchy," he said.

"What do you mean?"

"Well, in ACT UP," he explained "we were all in it together. What was important was that you did your work. In the theater culture, the way it is now, it's the opposite. Everything is based on where you sit on the totem pole. It has nothing to do with how interesting your vision is, how good an artist you are, or even if they like you or not. People are brutally cruel to you if you have less currency, and repulsively solicitous if you have more. That's the only operating principle."

He was describing the heart of supremacy ideology, in which people get ignored and disrespected, or attended to and praised based entirely on their social positioning. In a direct mirror of gentrification values, the theater is investing boring corporate and homogenized aesthetics with meaning that they do not hold, simply because dominant culture people are creating it.

Over the subsequent years I have slowly come to understand that he was not exaggerating. This description, the world he evokes, is accurate. I understand that theater is particularly vulnerable to bad values because of its proximity to movie stars, and the regular interactions between theater artists who can't earn a living and those who make obscene amounts of money that they don't deserve. This brush with money is corrupting, of course, and coupled with the high percentage of theater folks who live on inherited wealth, makes the environment lethal. The other obstacle, I think, is that theater is an elite art form, not a mass art form like book publishing. Not-for-profit subscription theaters that rarely move productions to Broadway really only need to sell a limited number of tickets. So, they don't need to expand the kinds of people they reach and serve. And since there is no checks and balances system, they don't feel accountable to the broad range of human perspectives. But still, the horrible way people are treated in this contemporary theater world has nothing to do with what I learned about being an artist, or the values I picked up over the years about making art. What is the difference between my disappeared world and this current gentrified regime?

Looking really closely, the most significant factor differentiating the disappeared avant-garde, destroyed by AIDS and gentrification, and the replacement artists, more closely aligned with the social structures necessary to be able to pay contemporary real estate prices, is professionalization. MFA programs. Especially MFA programs as markers of caste and brand. I came of age in the East Village in the 1980s. The freaky, faggy, outrageous, community-based, dangerous, "criminal class" was of course not the only influence, but they were a huge influence. Yes there were trust fund babies slumming, et cetera, but many artists I knew and learned from had an outlaw quality. They had illegal sex, took illegal drugs, hustled literally and figuratively for money, lived in poverty, and said *fuck you* to dominant cultural values, all of which made it possible for them to discover new art ideas later enjoyed by the world. Many of them died or became marginalized. And they, in part, were replaced by people who were trained in and graduated from expensive institutions. The "Downtown" that I was raised in as a young artist included real innovators, real drag queens, real street dykes, real refugees, real Nuyoricans, really inappropriate risk-taking, sexually free nihilistic utopians. Today, "Downtown" means having an MFA from Brown.

Some of them are good writers, and I'm thankful for that. But the larger cultural point is that the homogeneity of preparation, combined with the lack of opportunity for those not institutionally produced, results in an American theater profoundly complicit with *and a tool of* the dominant apparatus—which is the opposite of what should be if it is to provide an alternative to corporate thinking.

I remember kind of realizing this trend somewhere about five years into curating the New York Lesbian and Gay Experimental Film Festival, which Jim and I founded in 1987, the same year that ACT UP began. At first we showed artists who were experimental. That is to say, they experimented. "Experimental" meant that each artist singularly tried out their own eccentric idea, their own imaginative way, and then they looked at each other's discoveries. They learned how to be artists by making art, talking about art, looking at art, being with artists. Whether or not one went to graduate school was irrelevant (and still is) to whether or not one was really an artist. But at some point around the height of AIDS/gentrification this shifted. Those true experimenters who needed to earn a living in the rapidly shifting gentrification economy were channeled by inflation into teaching jobs. The increasing number of MFA programs became the only way that artists could earn a living beyond waitressing or copyediting at night at law firms. MFA programs became workfare for writers, as rents skyrocketed, as arts funding—already so elite as to be culturally damaging—was practically eliminated. It was like the role of the artist in society had devolved from WPA to NEA to MFA. Their students started producing inside a now established genre called "experimental." It wasn't actually any longer experimental, but it was a fixed set of derivative paradigms, invented by their teachers—many of whom did not have MFAs.

The same thing happened in theater. Experimental discoverers like Anne Bogart, Richard Foreman, the Wooster Group started to spawn. Economics drove artists into the academy and schools began producing students working in motifs invented by their teachers. Paula Vogel, formerly at Brown, now running playwrighting at Yale School of Drama, was one such influential teacher. Her dreamlike, sometimes highly stylized humor intercut with heartbreaking emotional truths, entering in and out of "reality" and imagined universes, became a genre of theater. While some of her students are among my favorite playwrights, others replicate or enhance her aesthetic of whimsy without the hard-core need at the heart of her work. After all, the nature of that first wave of mandatory MFA programs is that some students are far more protected than their teachers were, and can embrace the aesthetic ideas without the cultural conflict evidenced, for example, in Vogel's most exciting plays. It's a variation on the theme of hardscrabble artists becoming the tutors of the bourgeoisie. I remember filmmaker Leslie Thornton talking about the issue of teaching students who had more money for their films than their professors did, what that felt like. Or poet Joan Larkin describing teaching at an elite college as, "Sit on my lap and write your novel my darling." Donald Margulies captured this irony in his play *Collected Stories*, in which a hardworking woman writer (slightly resembling Grace Paley) is forced to teach the children of the ruling class in order to earn a living. And not being of them, she misassesses them and their ruthlessness—treating them like young artists and not like the elites for whom she is actually a tutor instead of a mentor.

Of course now that the noose has tightened even further, civilian artists are systematically excluded from teaching, as having an MFA has become mandatory for hiring. Being a product of MFA acculturation is now more important in determining who will influence students than what that person has achieved artistically. So, the frame of information and impulse becomes even more narrow and irrelevant and its product even more banal.

The same thing happened in fiction, although it took a bit longer. Innovative teachers like Carole Maso, also at Brown, who had accrued an eclectic personal aesthetic, started producing students who were so entranced by the charisma of her work that I could read something and know that that person studied with Carole Maso at Brown. But that's the happy version. The yuppier, more boring teachers reproduced ruling-class pabulum among their students. Breezy journalistic sentences about wealthy white people unaware that other human beings are real became the rubber stamp product of the elite MFA programs. The rest of the heap—the programs that accept most of the people who apply—are often just money machines ripping off people who are not writers and will never be writers while paying starvation wages to the real writers teaching to survive. It's a Ponzi scheme. The kind of thing that sent Bernie Madoff to jail. I wonder how many graduates of MFA programs actually ever publish a book or have a real play production? My guess would be less than 5 percent.

I admit, I did think about getting an MFA once I learned what it was. I had never actually heard of one until I already had two books published, but as the art world around me started to gentrify I realized that an MFA was a necessary socialization if you wanted connections. It was like joining a gang—you had to be a Blood or a Crip or no one would have your back. So, I registered at the City College of New York, and—not even realizing that they offered an MA, not an MFA—I set off for my first day of class. When I got there, the teacher was Grace Paley. A great writer who did not have an MFA, but rather learned to write in her kitchen until she was read by an editor, who happened to live in the same building and was actually interested in literature instead of who knew who. The year this story takes place,

Grace was working three jobs. For that first day of class, she had us go around and read examples of our work out loud. I read a scene from my novel-in-progress *After Delores*, in which the lesbian narrator meets a little go-go dancer named Punkette, who takes her back to her tenement apartment and tells her about the woman she loves. I finished reading and it was time for the other students to offer their comments. It didn't take long for it to become very clear that the students thought the narrator was a man.

Oh no, I thought. *This is going to be two years of hell.*

After class, Grace looked at me.

"Come to my office," she said in that unreconstituted New York accent. "Look," she told me once the door was closed. "You're really a writer. You're really doing it. You don't need this class. Go home."

So I left and never went back. And she saved me.

But like many of my contemporaries I ended up teaching in an MFA program for fourteen years, and now I teach creative writing to undergraduates in the City University of New York. I got through the system on something that no longer exists called "professional equivalence," because I had already published eight books at the time of my CUNY appointment in 1999. Maybe nine out of my entire lifetime of writing students are real writers, and I would have helped them anyway. Most of my students have had some kind of personal growth experience that has benefited them as human beings through the work and conversations, but that is more about a kind of therapy and not at all about the process of becoming an artist.

These developments gentrify cultural production, homogenize what kinds of artists and artwork win approval, and further alienate the rest of the population from having a real shot.

What counterindicates professionalization programs from real art-making are some key differences.

- One is the homogenization of influences. Students in an MFA program often are exposed to the same ideas and artworks as their classmates. They don't stumble through the world accruing eclectic influences, based on their own aesthetic interests, impulses, and chance. They lose the opportunity to fight to be influenced, to check out weird things and trail after unusual people. This creates homogeneity.

- Second, the process of going to school, the admission selection and the high cost, is itself an enormous filter, reducing who will ultimately have the access an MFA provides. This is further homogenizing the field. Graduate programs are filtered communities, the world is not.

- Third—and the most obnoxious—some MFA students and recent grads become focused on a concept of mainstream success that is predicated on the repetition of what is already known. Before they even achieve anything, many are already involved in the lifestyle of being mean to people who don't have their pedigree and solicitous to those who do. There is an overemphasis on positioning one's self and a grotesque lack of interest in real discussion about art and art-making, a lack of desire to grapple with something that matters, and to face one's self realistically in an honest representation of the real world, lived and imagined. I am consistently surprised at the almost complete lack of discussion about the ideology and values of a play. Critics don't bring it up and artists rarely discuss it. What does each specific play stand for? What is it rendering generic? What is it presenting as neutral? What is it saying about the consequences of experience? The prevailing ideology of the American theater is that the coming of age of the white male is the central and most important story in the culture. Most theaters are rigidly and dogmatically fixed in this idea. And when plays by "others" are allowed to be seen, the extent to which they are praised and rewarded often depends on the extent to which they reflect white males' desire to be seen in a particular light. While never made explicit, as MFA programs prime writers for reward, the message of what kinds of content and points of view are acceptable is clearly articulated. There is an unartful reliance on the cues of the exterior world, an engagement with values that place familiarity over expansion of consciousness.

· Finally, the payoff of getting an MFA, the reward for paying that bribe in a sense, is that if the person was obedient enough, they can be helped for the rest of their career by their teachers and mentors behind the scenes. The fact of having graduated from a program creates the possibility of a kind of professional opportunity that a civilian cannot access because the institution becomes invested in their graduates doing well. It gives graduates a false sense of pride because they had certain advantages, and makes them treat people like themselves as though their work matters simply because they went to a specific school.

Despite the fact that these programs are homogenizing and corrupting and bad for the culture, I feel that when I am advising working-class or poor students with talent, I have to insist that they go to them. There is simply no other way of getting into the system. As damaging as these programs are when they codify or elevate ruling-class perspectives and middlebrow practitioners, they become the only hope for outsiders to have a chance to be let in. It's a conundrum. Hopefully a talented person can emerge from these programs without a highly distorted sense of their own importance, and if they come originally from the margins this is more likely. But as far as I can see, MFA programs have done nothing to break down the barrier that full-character plays with authorial universes (not performance art, vaudeville, or stand-up) and authentic lesbian protagonists face in the theatrical marketplace. So although they do help certain minority voices who have had the support and sophistication to access and survive the system, overall they reinforce the dominant cultural voice, the clubbiness and repetition and most importantly, the group mentality that is, itself, counterindicated for art making.

Because of the severe censorship facing lesbian representation in the United States, and the added obstruction MFA programs have laid on lesbian writers who have both gravitas and lesbian protagonists, I decided to try, in my own way, to take a small action to counter the exclusions of the MFA process. In June 2008 I started a project I call "The Satellite Academy." This is composed of two monthly writing workshops I run out of my apartment for a small number of talented women writers (and one gay man) who are not enrolled in any academic program. In one class, most of the students are over forty and many are writing about the AIDS era. In the other most of my students are younger, queer in some way, the group is interracial, and all of my students enact some kind of bohemian or oppositional value in the way they live their lives. They are not institutional products. I charge forty dollars a class. I find that this does not take up much of my time—two days and evenings per month—and that I love my students. I adore them. I believe in them. I see in them the kinds of artists that I came up with. In my class they don't have to defend queerness, aesthetic invention, or racial or cultural points of view. And they don't have to take out loans. Once the burden of defending is reduced we can concentrate on craft. They get the same experience as the dominant culture writer in an MFA program: their lives are assumed to be important. And that's what we do. There is no chit-chat, no nurturing, no consciousness raising or eating. They come on time, and I take out my little blackboard and we go through each person's work with an eye towards craft alone. Much of the positioning, competing, explaining, paying tuition/loans, and defending that they would have to do in MFA programs is removed. We're artists together, looking at each other's work, and I am the senior one sharing what I know. In this way, I have recreated my lost world for myself, and it gives me hope that bohemian, smart angry girls with something new to say and a desire to say it are never in short supply. They're just being ignored by the gentrification of creation. But believe me, that's only temporary. My students will be heard—but only in a postgentrification world.

My dream is that other queer and nondominant culture writers, regardless of what they have to do for a living, will join the Satellite Academy and start their own groups. I remember in the seventies there used to be these radical alternative schools, like The University of the Streets, Brecht Forum, New York Jazz Coalition, and other rogue places of learning where people could take classes for minimal cost with teachers who really knew. If there were twenty low-cost classes a month in New York City for radical/queer/women writers, that would be enough of a critical mass to counteract the censorious impact of MFA programs. One hundred radical students in low-income writing classes in New York City could actually have an impact on our literature. And, it can help those of us who are good teachers and need to work for a living, to realize that while we need jobs to survive, we don't always need institutions in order to teach. We can just do it. Like we always did, before gentrification made us forget who we were.

CHAPTER FIVE

The Gentrification of Gay Politics

Election Day, November 2008. It's a new dawn for America. Barack Obama has triumphed at the polls and every constituency of people without rights in this country is united in the hope and determination that our system can work for them. Except one. While most of America is literally cheering, literally dancing *in the streets,* tears streaming down their faces, thirty-six thousand gay people who got married in California are devastated. On the same date that Obama was elected, four state ballot measures passed banning gay marriage, and two of those states—California and Florida—went for Obama. Arkansas, the political home of Bill Clinton, voted in a ballot measure banning gays and lesbians from being foster parents or adopting children. Over the next few days, the details begin to emerge. Barack Obama agreed with Hillary Clinton, John McCain, Sarah Palin, and George Bush as they all united in their opposition to gay marriage. Obama even went so far as to say that, "God ordained marriage to be between one man and one woman." This was the recorded message that Christian activists played over their telephones endlessly to California voters.

Truly spontaneous demonstrations explode in LA and San Francisco. They were not organized by the marriage leaders, who were immediately under scrutiny, but instead were fueled by young people who had believed the phony hype that gays and lesbians had equality. They were shocked at this defeat, revealing how truly effective the placating propaganda had been. It is quickly understood that 70 percent of Black voters in California voted against gay marriage. Racist grumblings start to emerge from white gays who overlook that Blacks are only 6 percent of the state's population. It becomes clear that the pro-gay marriage campaign did almost no appropriate outreach to Asian, Black, and Latino voters, and that Black and Latino and Asian gays and lesbians were not at the forefront of the campaign. Most importantly, it becomes clear that it was white voters who killed gay marriage in California, despite a great deal of white gay rage focused on Blacks and Latinos. Analysis of the marriage campaigners' organizing materials becomes even more acute. Apparently, few of the expensive television spots encouraging pro-gay voters to vote "No On Proposition 8" featured actual gay people talking about their own rights. Most of the ads featured parents of gays, friends of gays, young straight people proclaiming how proud they were to get married in a state where "everyone" has marriage rights. But gay people themselves were almost invisible in their own forty million dollar campaign.

While some gay communities are angry, frightened, alienated, and hurt by these political events, straight progressives are barely aware that any of this has happened. They warn us not to "ruin" the Obama moment, and inform us that "the economy is more important." It starts to be strangely clear after only a few weeks of Obama-elect that we have returned to a state of mind not seen for thirty years, in which straight people—Black and white and Latino, progressive and reactionary—are all suddenly convinced that gays and lesbians are white, bourgeois, privileged, and therefore fine to be sacrificed for the "greater good." Thirty years of work by gay people of color in all communities is suddenly undone by political expediency. Six months later, on the very day that Obama appoints the first Puerto Rican Supreme Court justice, Sonia Sotomayor, the California Supreme Court upholds Proposition 8 by a vote of six to one. For the second time, a major victory for racial equality corresponds to a significant defeat for full gay personhood. One hundred demonstrations are organized around the country, but most are rather dutiful and benign.

How did this happen? How did the gay liberation movement, which Black Panther Party Chairman Huey P. Newton once said "may be the most revolutionary" . . . a movement whose slogans were "Smash the family, smash the state" and "An army of lovers cannot fail" . . . a group relationship that envisioned total revolution of gender and sex roles, social accountability, and community-based responsibility . . . a community that faced the AIDS crisis with unity and endless imagination . . . how did this radical, living, creative force get excluded from Obama's freedom vision and deteriorate into a group of racist, closeted, top-down privatized couples willing to sacrifice their entire legacy to get married? And fail?

Before we blame ourselves entirely for our own deterioration, we must remember that the loss of vision gay people have experienced since the election of Ronald Reagan in 1980 is partially a reflection of the dumbing down of American culture across the board. Americans' ignorance of and alienation from the rest of the world was accompanied by the narrowing of discourse, the homogenization of our cities, the restrictions on public conversation, the stupidity of American entertainment, and the gathering of power into fewer and fewer hands. Gay people are just Americans after all, and it is hard to retain independent consciousness and awareness when being bombarded by reactionary culture. Yet, the decline of revolutionary thinking by gays and lesbians has its own special trajectory that is dynamic with American decline, but also specific to our own history.

I think it is obvious, though unexplored, that this terrible moment of lost vision is a consequence not only of America's lost vision but also of the unexplored impact of the AIDS crisis on the gay and lesbian self. Contextualize this with the homogenization of cities where gays and lesbians' political imaginations once thrived. And most importantly, with the relationship between these two events: the unexplored trauma of the AIDS crisis, and the loss of the radical culture of mixed urbanity. Set it all against the backdrop of the Reagan/Bush years, and we discover how we got here. To a place where homosexuality loses its own transformative potential and strives instead to be banal.

If you ask most people what the most pressing issue for queers is in America today, they will say "marriage." Inherent in this is the assumption that everything else is great for gay people, and only marriage remains. Yet there is no nationwide antidiscrimination law, and marginalization in publicly-funded institutions like schools and the New York City Saint Patrick's Day parade is firmly in place. There is no integration of lesbians of all races or gay men of color's perspectives into mainstream arts or entertainment. Familial homophobia is the status quo. We are not integrated into education curriculum or services. Being out is professionally detrimental in most fields. Most heterosexuals still think of themselves as superior and most gay people submit to this out of necessity or lack of awareness. Basically, in relation to where we should be—we are nowhere.

But how did we get nowhere, when it looked like we were doing so well? This is a question I would like to begin to look at in this chapter, realizing that it is bigger than me. All I can do is start with my own perception that one of the key moments where we lost momentum of vision was when our leadership transitioned from organic to appointed. That is to say, when we shifted from leaders who rose naturally from within our communities to ones who were appointed by corporate media, and subsequently by corporate donations.

Donald Suggs once said to me, "The drag queens who started Stonewall are no better off today, but they made the world safe for gay Republicans. It's a bitter pill to swallow, but the people who make change are not the people who benefit from it."

The AIDS crisis made gay people visible. For the first time we were on prime-time news programs, in newspapers, while dying and death made the closet more difficult to maintain. I've gone into this process in depth in my book *Stagestruck: Theater, AIDS and the Marketing of Gay America*, but in short, the visibility created by AIDS forced the dominant group to change their stance. They could no longer insist that homosexuality did not exist. What they could do is find representative homosexuals with whom they were comfortable, and integrate them into some realm of public conversation. If they didn't, the gay voice in America would be people with AIDS disrupting mass at Saint Patrick's Cathedral. It was crucial to the containment crisis that acceptable gay personalities be identified and positioned as "leaders," even if they had no grassroots base. It's kind of like the CIA setting up a puppet government.

This is a classic gentrification event. Authentic gay community leaders, who have been out and negotiating/fighting/uniting/dividing with others for years, the people who have built the formations and institutions of survival, become overlooked by the powers that be. They are too unruly, too angry, too radical in their critique of heterosexism, too faggy, too sexual. The dominant culture would have to change in order to accommodate them. And most importantly they are telling the truth about heterosexual cruelty. The dominant culture needed gay people who would pathologize their own. Supremacy ideology could not tolerate the confrontation with the heterosexual self that is at the core of gay liberation. So instead of the representative radicals, there was an unconscious but effective search for palatable individuals with no credibility in the community, no accountability to anyone, with no history of bravery or negotiation with other queers, who were then appointed in their stead. This replacement process, facilitated by the straight media, really became visible in the late nineties. It was the first time that I noticed a crew of guys being interviewed on television as emblematic gay men whom I had never seen in a community capacity. It was the moment when the corporate media was creating its own gay personalities, who were entirely different from the people featured in the gay-owned press. And eventually, the grassroots voices were drowned out completely, as gentrification co-opted the gay media, and the gay liberation movement, dialogically, was demobilized.

In 1998, I interviewed two white males from opposite sides of the divide for the *Advocate*, which had long been the most conservative national gay news publication. Rooted in the California community and initially funded by sex ads, the *Advocate* had just recently volunteered to relegate all sexual advertising to a pull-out section in exchange for an ad campaign from Absolut Vodka, the first mainstream company to niche market its product to gay consumers. While the *Advocate* had steadfastly refused to cover women (I remember the editor, Jeff, asking me who Allison Bechdel was), they also refused to racially integrate, insisting that every time they put a nonwhite male on the cover, their sales dropped. This was always an indicator to me of who their readers were. Ironically, the *Advocate* was being outrun by *Out* magazine, the truly gentrified publication, who didn't put gay people on the cover at all. They were more nihilistic than conservative, as they were motivated entirely by marketing. *Out* did not cover gay politics with any depth, and instead focused on consumer products their readers could be niche-marketed to buy. It could probably be categorized as the first openly gay magazine for the blasé and their friends.

Yet in this weird transitional moment, 1998, I was invited (possibly because lesbians had come into editorial leadership after a long line of dead and ill male editors) to conduct interviews with Edmund White and Andrew Sullivan for the *Advocate*'s pages. Although both men are white, of a certain age, HIV-positive, and identified with certain class-based pleasures, Edmund White and Andrew Sullivan came from opposite sides of the gay tracks.

Here I want to replicate some excerpts from these two conversations because their juxtaposition illuminates the difference between the two points of view, and hopefully will make clear why Sullivan ended up as the chosen corporate mass media spokesperson for the gay community and White did not.

HE OUTLIVED HIS DEATH:
INTERVIEW WITH EDMUND WHITE

s: The title of your new novel *Farewell Symphony* and its cataloguing of your life and loves implies that you may have expected to die of AIDS before its publication. Now that you are hopefully outliving your own death, how do you feel about having thrown caution to the wind?

EW: I started it as my last book. I've always been a charming writer who depended upon charm both in life and in work. I didn't want to be quite so seductive and I didn't mind showing myself in an unattractive light.

s: Do you feel that the waning sense of crisis around gay men and AIDS has left a community that has miraculously "coped" or is there a fury, despair, and regret waiting to be unleashed?

EW: I think there will be people over thirty now who have survived and who will feel themselves becoming more and more marginalized by younger people who aren't as aware of the whole battle. That's going to be painful in a very different way. It's one thing to think that we all went through this together and survived it and "here's my story of what I went through." It's going to be another thing to have nobody want to read those stories.

s: *Farewell Symphony* was trashed by Larry Kramer in the *Advocate* for representing your promiscuity. Your novel *Caracole* was obstructed by Susan Sontag because she saw herself unflatteringly depicted. What do you

feel when powerful people try to hurt you
professionally?

EW: In both cases they were friends so I felt betrayed. I
had sent Larry proofs of the book. In the manuscript
I claimed that I was the one who invented the name
Gay Men's Health Crisis [for the organization White
cofounded]. Larry called up and said, "I think it was
me and I've told all the historians it was me, could you
please change that?" and I said "Fine." Otherwise all he
said to me was, "Ed, Ed you did not have all that sex."
And I said "But Larry, I did." Then the next thing I know
there's this explosion, choosing me as a focal point for his
diatribe. "Sucking cock in the bushes, is that all we are?
What about Tolstoy, Flaubert?" And so on. Forgetting
that Tolstoy and Flaubert had enormous scandals on
their hands. Flaubert had an obscenity trial. Why didn't
Larry call me and talk it over? He misrepresented me
and he misrepresented *The Joys of Gay Sex*, which came
out in 1978, not on the "eve" of the health crisis. And even
if it had, I'm not a crystal ball reader and nobody in 1980
would have known that in 1981 there was going to be the
AIDS virus.

People said to me, "It's good. It's controversy. It's going
to sell copies." But I didn't feel that at all. I just feel angry
and then kind of wounded. I respect Susan Sontag a lot
more than I do Larry Kramer, as a mind and as a person.
So, when I had my run-in with her, I really didn't expect
that she would react that way to my book. First of all, if
she had kept her own mouth shut no one would have ever
recognized her. Only she would have recognized herself
because it's not a roman à clef. It takes place in another

century, another country. I based the character half on Madame de Staël. To the degree that every writer has to find some models for their characters, I did that too but it was anything but a direct attack on her. We were very close for a long time and I still have dreams that she and I will become friends again. But Larry, I just wash my hands of it.

s: Although you've maintained a WASP patrician image, you've always been open about your sexual history and desires. Hustlers, unsafe sex, masochism, phone sex, enemas, and endless tricking. Yet this stands in contrast to a number of white gay men who have been calling for marriage and monogamy. Is this the time for gay people to adapt heterosexual mores?

EW: No. First of all, about my image. I never quite know what that comes from. My parents were both Texans, my mother never wore shoes until she was sixteen. I went to the University of Michigan, not Harvard. I never got a single penny from anybody. The minute I graduated college I was completely on my own. I'm earning one hundred percent of my living from my pen. Being seen as a patrician has to do with the way I talk or act or look or something, but it has nothing to do with the social realities. I've always struggled to make a living.

In terms of monogamy, I think that's absurd. People who are ranting in that way are going to lose all credibility with younger people. To say to some twenty-year-old gay man, "you should become monogamous" is crazy since what they really want is a lot of sex. I have always seen gay life as an alternative to straight life.

If gay life meant just reproducing straight life, I'd rather be a monk.

What makes White typical of community-based figures are some key elements revealed in his interview. He has always been out. He is self-aware. He has a history with activist organizing, while maintaining his individuality as an artist. He thinks in terms of the community, recognizes its trends and changes. He is available and accountable to the community, and as a consequence has had those kinds of difficult moments that accountable people experience, particularly in a longtime conflict with Larry Kramer over the very question of sexual freedom. The simple expectation that Larry Kramer should have called him up and talked over their differences shows that White values accountability and negotiation with other human beings. Most significantly, he believes in a gay male sexual culture that is not the same as heterosexual culture.

INTERVIEW WITH ANDREW SULLIVAN

The interview began with an extensive discussion of Sullivan's new book *Love Undetectable*, that is not reproduced here. Then the conversation turned to other questions. Here are some excerpts:

s: Do you believe that life begins at conception?

AS: Where in the book does this come up?

s: No, I'm asking you.

AS: It's like you have a set of PC questions.

s: It is relevant because you are a spokesperson for the gay and lesbian community, you are one of the few

in the gay and lesbian community who have access to
the mainstream media and a huge amount of visibility.
There are a lot of people in this community who are
very interested in things like abortion. You do put your
Catholicism front and center, and I think it is a perfectly
reasonable question.

AS: I do too. Every question is reasonable. It's just, you know
. . . asking about how I fit into leftist orthodoxy.

S: Okay, so do you want to pass?

AS: No, I'll answer your question.

S: Are you in favor of a repeal of *Roe v. Wade*?

AS: Yes.

S: Do you endorse and vote for antiabortion candidates?

AS: I can't vote and I don't endorse candidates.

S: But you did endorse the Human Rights Campaign support
for Alphonse D'Amato for U.S. Senate from New York.

AS: Absolutely. But I'm not in favor of making abortion
illegal tomorrow. And I'm not in favor of a constitutional
amendment to make it illegal. And I have taken a very
strong stance against pro—alleged pro-life terrorism.
And I do think, certainly within the first trimester there
is such a deep division of moral belief. The people who
disagree with me have such an integrity to their views
that I would not make it illegal for someone to have an
abortion in the first trimester ever. I may disagree with
them about what is moral, but in a culture such as ours I
would tolerate that. I still think it's wrong, and still could
not myself be a party to it in any way. But I would defend
the right of someone to go ahead, given how genuinely
divided our culture is on this matter. That makes a kind

of pro-choice pro-lifer. Which is where I think a lot of people are.

s: Are you involved in grassroots organizing on the marriage question?

AS: Well, it depends on what you mean by that. If you mean, have I, you know, gone to cities and talked about it and raised money and talked to anybody who wants to talk to me about it, yes.

s: But not just as Andrew Sullivan, spokesperson. I mean, your support for that issue is well known. But have you ever been involved in a community-based grassroots organization?

AS: I'm not a group person, I never have been.

s: You are the most visible gay person in the media of this country. You're on prime-time talk shows, you're in the *New York Times*. You're in the *Times* today. Are you surprised that you have become the token gay man who is represented in the media?

AS: I *[laughs]* don't, I'm not sure that's entirely true. There are many people out there talking about those things and I think it's flattering, what you said. . . . All I've ever done is write and defend my writing and if I'm asked to go on TV, I've gone on to defend whatever. I think you do that well or not well. Obviously they think that I can do it and so they've asked me back on. But you know, it's not really a question of access because it's really up to them.

s: Why do you think that they, meaning the media . . .

AS: Like the bookers, you know.

s: Why have they selected you?

AS: Well, they know that if I go on, I'm going to be reasonable and cogent.

S: But don't you see yourself as representing a minority opinion within the gay community?

AS: No, I don't think that at all. The vast majority agree with almost, with much of what I say. It is only a very small minority of people who really do feel threatened by certain arguments and ideas.

S: How do you assess that?

AS: Once upon a time, when the gay world was smaller, it was more easily controlled by a particular political faction. And it was monolithic. It has become more diverse. There are more variety of voices out here and the old elites are very threatened. So they attempt to demonize or stigmatize or marginalize people who they disagree with.

S: Okay, that's your scenario. Let me offer you mine and you tell me why I'm wrong. There are quite a few people who have come from the grassroots up and have built a community. They have a great deal of legitimacy within that community. But they have never been recognized by the dominant culture. They have never been offered a voice at the highest level. They are now watching people be selected whose views are most acceptable to the dominant group.

AS: You really think that arguing for same-sex marriage is most acceptable?

S: Well, what's the other argument?

AS: *[laughs]* I think it is the one argument that is most likely to provoke opposition, and the polls will tell you that.

s: Actually, my recollection is that before the AIDS crisis,
gay marriage was considered preposterous. But once there
was ACT UP doing things like going into Saint Patrick's
Cathedral . . .

AS: You think that made same-sex marriage more palatable.

s: Yes, absolutely.

AS: *[laughs]* I think that's ludicrous. AIDS, undoubtedly,
for a whole variety of reasons, brought gay and straight
Americans into a whole conversation and dialogue, and
because it reasserted the notion amongst many gay people
of our equality and our dignity, as I say in the book—that
marriage came to the fore naturally. Definitely, I'm not
out there telling straight America what it wants to hear. It
doesn't want to hear that we demand marriage rights.
It doesn't want to hear that we deserve to be equally in
the military.

s: But I think that that position is much more palatable than
a defense of a community-based culture, and a rejection
of privatized family units on a reproductive model. That's
what they don't want to hear. . . . What they do want to
hear . . .

AS: And that's what they love to hear. Gay people saying that.
Because it just means that gay people don't want to be
part of society, and they are very happy with that. There
is nothing the mainstream likes more than some person
standing up and saying, "We gay people reject all that
you stand for." They love that. That keeps us where we
belong as far as they are concerned.

s: I don't know, I watch my friends who are having children,
now, you know. The lesbian baby boom. And suddenly

their families who rejected them for twenty years
are welcoming them back in because they are fitting
some kind of model of motherhood. You know there has
been . . .

AS: You want them to stop doing that?

S: You said they reject us wanting to enter the society on
their terms. I say, no—the more we resemble their ideas
of how we should behave . . .

AS: It's a human model. It's not a heterosexual monopoly.
It is a human goal—to define ourselves by where we've
been instead of where we are going is demeaning to
gay people. I think I certainly don't. I'm not out there
to win a popularity contest. Even if you despise
everything I've ever written, you can't say I've sought
out popularity.

S: You've gotten a lot of approval from mainstream
culture.

AS: If that's true, then why do my books sell to the gay
community?

S: Your books? I don't know your sales exactly, but you
probably sell around thirty-five thousand copies. That is
the top-out for gay male books. Did you know that? I've
been in the gay book business for fifteen years and I can
tell you that that is the limit above which almost no one
speaking to gay people can go.

AS: But that does mean some gay people are buying my
books.

S: But it is the same amount of gay and straight people
combined who are buying other people's books. You claim
to represent this huge majority, but your sales are entirely

within the traditional framework of people who support
gay male writing. It's the gay market. I read your book but
not because I agree with you.

AS: *[laughs]* I haven't been selected by anybody. All I've done
is write and think and go out there.

S: But other people do that too. And they don't have the same
access. You know that, right?

AS: I don't know that. I think anybody can have access. I
didn't come with any particular, you know, privilege.
I don't understand what that means. Anybody who can
speak cogently and coherently and can write well can
have access, period.

S: Okay.

AS: And the notion that someone is somehow selecting
you because of some sinister cabal is absurd. And
you keep referring to extreme leftists as "the
community." *[laughs]* They're not the community.
They are not. They represent tiny fractions of gay
people in this country. We know from exit polls that
33 percent of gay people voted Republican in 1998.
Imagine that's underreporting. Forty percent are voting
Republican. Are they not the community? Where do they
come from?

S: Okay.

AS: They are the people who are being marginalized by
the old elites. The old gay elites who want to keep their
power and are losing it.

S: What power?

AS: The power to define who is gay or not.

s: All those people did was give their lives to building a movement that made it possible for people like you to come out.

AS: Nonsense.

s: Oh, come on.

AS: *[laughs]* I came out because I came out.

s: No, a social context was created in which you could come out.

AS: Believe me, I should be able to say why I came out. The existence of an extreme left wing of gay people as the representation of gay people prevented me from coming out. It prevents other people from coming out, because they do not feel that that is them. In fact, if they have to be quote unquote queer, then they're not going to come out. In fact, the establishment of these left-wing elites actually impedes the possibility of gay people living fulfilled lives. It keeps them back in the ghettos. In my view, the gay movement was hijacked in the late seventies, in the seventies.

s: By street activists.

AS: Yes.

s: So, in your view, Stonewall was the downfall of the gay movement.

AS: Yes, it was definitely a diversion from the capacity of gay integration into our society.

s: Let me ask you one final question. Exactly how do you think change gets made?

AS: It gets made every time a human being stands up in whatever context for a principle that makes sense to them.

> It doesn't have to be in a movement or politics. In the
> words of Robert Kennedy, when one person stands up
> against injustice, in whatever way it is.

Even twelve years later, this interview is stunning on so many
levels. It is an illustration of classic supremacy ideology. First,
Mr. Sullivan does not understand that he is being elevated by a
structure of domination. He believes that the selection system
is neutral and merit based, and that he naturally rises to the top
because of his superiority. He sees no relationship between the
content of his argument and the reward of access. The second,
most indelible element of supremacy ideology is also present—
feeling oppressed by being asked to be accountable. He is offended
that I think it notable that he opposes abortion beyond the first
trimester. He is angry that his opposition to *Roe v. Wade* would be of
concern. He laughs repeatedly and says that I am "PC"—the classic supremacy response to demands of accountability—because
I don't want a corporate media-appointed representative of gay
people who is antiabortion. The third, ever-present element of
supremacy ideology is the false construction of powerful people
as victimized by their subordinates. He claims that gay Republicans who voted for George H. W. Bush are oppressed by those
of us who created all the foundational structures of service and
acknowledgement that form the base of the gay community: the
newspapers, the advocacy organizations, the activist movement,
the social services, the daring to have essential public conversations even if they are met with disrespect—so that the basic paradigms of our existence can be articulated. And that he himself
is oppressed by out gays, that it is us, and not homophobes or his
family who kept him in the closet. He is offended at being asked
to be accountable and he is incapable of thinking about himself

in an analytical way, claiming that change comes from vague individual gestures without context. And finally, history has proven that gay marriage is dramatically more acceptable to the tolerance model than any true equality concept of distinct culture or community-based structure. In the end though, the fact that Mr. Sullivan is still alive and healthy is a direct consequence of the AIDS activist movement, and owes nothing to folks who, like himself, claim to "not be a group person."

Just for the sake of historical corrective, I want to excerpt a bit here from my 2007 interview in the *Harvard Gay and Lesbian Review* with Marcia Gallo about her book *Different Daughters: A History of the Daughters of Bilitis and the Rise of the Lesbian Rights Movement.* I certainly don't want anyone coming away from my book without an accurate concept of who these early radicals were and how they built the movement in groups. These principled men and women made the sacrifice of being the shock troops willing to be out—they created the context for others, in the future, to become openly gay television pundits, despite gay Republicans.

THE DAUGHTER OF THE DAUGHTERS OF BILITIS: INTERVIEW WITH MARCIA GALLO

s: It was fascinating to discover in your book that the first lesbian organization was interracial from the first day in 1955.

MG: There were interracial couples in DOB [Daughters of Bilitis], so white women were dealing with women of color on an intimate level. It was always a struggle. Some of them tried really hard to ensure interracial involvement and some of them didn't, but the

consciousness was there. Which was one of the reasons I
fell in love with these folks. I think that the idea of racial
discrimination was very understood on a gut level, it
wasn't theoretical. They were influenced by people like
Eleanor Roosevelt and A. Philip Randolph. They paid
attention to racial struggles. They borrowed from the
civil rights movement over and over again.

But if you actually read their publication, *The Ladder*,
it's not there. They took on race only as an example of
a way for lesbians and gay men to assert their claims for
equal rights. So, you don't see stories about the March
on Washington per se, you see references to learning
from the civil rights movement. They were the first to
put women of color on the cover, but only three or four
times in fourteen years. And the one African American
president of DOB, in 1963—she was the first person of
color to lead a gay or lesbian civil rights group—so
far as I know remained pretty low key. So, fifty years
of trying to deal with racism on a personal as well as
organizational level. But that they struggled was what
was so fascinating to me. Not that they were righteous.
They would engage in these critical conversations
about practice as well as politics. About racism, about
separatism versus working with men, about trans issues.

s: I love your perspective. You write about regular people
who changed the world and ask about their various
relationships to power. This is how a few generations
of lesbians and feminists were trained to think. Yet
in the contemporary moment, this point of view is
most often mocked. If you think of dominant culture
characterizations of a lesbian perspective, asking who

has the power is considered to be a drag, humorless, ideological. Special interest, instead of as an organic, enlightened point of view.

MG: Feminism is still subversive. It's still scary. Feminism means humanity moving forward and addressing inequalities. And that women lead. Independent women who do not need men for their emotional, physical, and economic well being are scary still. Even those of us who love men. I think that the fact that we strive to be independent is frightening because we challenge all the paradigms. When we're at our best we challenge the way power gets constructed. We challenge how knowledge is transmitted. We are just too powerful, too uncontrollable, too queer.

CHAPTER SIX

The Gentrification of Our Literature

The first gay book I ever saw was called *Cycle Suck*. It was on a shelf at the Oscar Wilde Bookstore on Christopher Street in 1975, next to some mimeographed pamphlets with titles like "The Woman-Identified Woman." From the beginning, I have always known that this is as it should be. Separating distinctions between the sexually explicit and the politically necessary would never make sense. Yet, as I am writing this in 2009, a scandal erupts—first online and then in the mainstream print media. Amazon.com, the mail order bookseller mega-monster, got caught in what it called a "glitch." In response to right-wing and Christian readers, Amazon removed books with sexual content from its ranking system, thereby ensuring that erotic and pornographic books would not be able to get on best-seller lists. Either deliberately or inadvertently, gay and lesbian books were included in the ban and so were automatically removed from the Amazon ranking system. This included some editions of all of my books. The response of the gay community was tepid at best. A number of spokespeople called upon by the mainstream media or speaking out on Facebook and various blogs were "shocked" and "outraged" (see above responses to the passing of Proposition 8). They couldn't believe this was happening to them. The event was treated as an anomaly, irregular and extreme. When it was made clear that these exclusions included James Baldwin novels, the outrage grew. How could "literature" be confused with pornography?

For me, Amazon's actions were consistent with the way gay and lesbian literature has been contextualized in the United States. It is the surprise of some gay people and the pretend "mistake" of a media/industry that consistently marginalizes our work as a matter of course, that constitute the gentrified approach. As disenfranchised people often do the dirty work of the culture, we—gay, lesbian, bisexual (not yet transgendered, but that phenomena is inevitable) writers—gentrify ourselves. In the past, power brokers would not pretend that gay books were included when they were in fact excluded, and therefore susceptible gay people would not think that their work was included when it was in fact demeaned. The public explanation has changed, but the reality remains the same. The truth—that queer, sexually truthful literature is seen as pornographic, and is systematically kept out of the hands and minds of most Americans, gay and straight—has been replaced with a false story of a nonexistent integration and a fantasized equality, with no basis in lived fact. Truth is replaced by falsity, the false claim that the dominant culture writer does not have profound structural advantages replaces the truth that being out in one's work, sexually honest, and truthful about the lived homosexual experience guarantees that one's work will never be seen for its actual merit. The gentrified mind becomes unable to see lived experience because it is being bombarded by false stories. Even we, the practitioners, cannot understand the truthful positioning of our literature. In short, to be acceptable, literature cannot be sexually authentic. And, even though this is a requirement for approval, we look at the highly conditional and restricted approval as a sign of success instead of the failure that it actually is.

In my own experience, the equation of queer literature with pornography is undeniable. Yes, this includes the banning of condom ads on television. Of course, in gay time, "recent" quickly disappears because so many participants are dead, and others have been silenced. It's hard to have collective memory when so many who were "there" are not "here" to say what happened. Once the recent past is remembered, then the Amazon "glitch" becomes all too consistent. So, here is just one example exhumed from memory.

In 1994, a coalition of feminists and right-wing politicians in Canada passed a tariff code called Butler that was designed to restrict pornographic production. Instead, it was applied in such a way that it allowed officials at Canada customs to systematically detain and destroy gay and lesbian materials at the border. A gay bookstore in Vancouver, Little Sisters, had so much of its product seized at the border that it could no longer operate. As a result, Little Sisters decided to sue the Canadian government.

My friend John Preston had just died of AIDS. He was the author of some iconic leather and S/M novels, many with literary bent. His novel *Mister Benson* had been serialized in *Drummer* magazine, and created a subcultural phenomena. Men would wear T-shirts asking *Mister Benson?* Or asserting *Mister Benson!* While he had a less explicit series called *Franny, the Queen of Provincetown,* John was perhaps best known for his book *I Once Had a Master.* Since he was newly dead, I was asked by the Little Sisters legal team to come to Vancouver and testify on John's behalf. And because I was very clear in my opposition to state repression of gay materials, I had no problem agreeing.

The Canadian courthouse was quite shocking to this New Yorker. No metal detectors, no armed guards at rapt attention in every corner. The building looked like a Marriott hotel, with lovely plants, comfortable seating, and a coffee bar. But do not be fooled, the Canadian government proved to be a vicious animal with a demure exterior.

Tensions were high in the courtroom the day I arrived. The trial had been going on for weeks and many writers had testified. Patrick Califia, who at the time had presented as female with the name Pat, had been on the witness stand the Friday before and had done so well that the Crown had refused to cross-examine him. Interestingly, "Pat"—who was known as a butch leather dyke—had taking the extreme step of wearing a brown corduroy dress, which impressed me. We were, after all, trying to win. I, and I assume many of the women testifying, had agonized over what to wear on the stand. The only nice dress I owned in 1994 was black velvet—kind of a parody of a dress, and something to be worn to the opera. Anyway, I wore pants. Becky Ross, a Canadian academic, testified before me. She wore a dress, but I think she always wore a dress. Anyway, the Crown had been pretty hard on her, asking her to define "fisting."

John's books were being persecuted on five counts. The questions I had to address were: Is it violent? Is it degrading? Is it dehumanizing? Does it have literary merit? Is it socially redeeming? If I had had my way, I would have argued that even if the books were violent, degrading, et cetera, they still should be available. However, Canadian courts had already ruled on that question, so my only remaining strategy for protecting his books was to "prove" that Butler should not be applied to him. Not that the law was wrong.

So many years later, this is the same conundrum gay writers faced with the Amazon exclusion. Mark Doty, Larry Kramer, and many other principled gay writers noted online and in print that books like *Giovanni's Room* and *Oranges Are Not the Only Fruit* were being falsely labeled as pornography. Once again we were forced by a state or corporate apparatus to claim that our literature was different from that dirty stuff, instead of part and parcel with it. But it is the homosexuality that got the books marginalized in the first place. Not their sentence structure.

If my editor will permit me, I would like to reproduce my court affidavit here. It may be the only chance most of you have to learn something about John, and that would please me greatly.

TESTIMONY ON BEHALF
OF JOHN PRESTON, VANCOUVER, 1994

I, Sarah Miriam Schulman, have had an opportunity to review John Preston's books *I Once Had a Master* and *Entertainment for a Master*. After consulting the legal principles by which the Supreme Court of Canada determines whether a book is obscene, I can say without reservation that these books are not obscene.

The first question is whether or not these books "contain explicit sex with violence." It seems clear that there is no physical violation of characters, only mutually consensual sexual relationships. Furthermore, none of these consensual sex acts result in physical impairment or injury. Nor is there any threat of physical violence in his work, only the *pretense* of such threat as an essential part of the fantasy surrounding these mutually consensual sex acts. At all times the characters are aware that they are participating in a sexual/emotional interaction by their own choice and motivated by their own desires. Never do the characters appear to be victims of violence or in fear of actual violence. The only violation is a social kind experienced by gay men who are shunned or ostracized by the dominant culture purely because of their homosexuality.

The second question has to do with "explicit sex which is degrading or dehumanizing." It is without a doubt that the characters in John's books feel emotionally and sexually enhanced by their relationships. His characters maintain dignity and sense of humor, and find an increasing awareness of community and self-esteem through their relationships with other men. In fact, their relationships are often positioned as a curative or solution to a feeling of degradation imposed on them by the non-gay world. Their relationships with other men are the very experiences that uplift John's characters from feelings of ostracization and rejection. Both books in question suggest that depriving people of information and images of their own emotional/sexual realities is an act of degradation, while affirming these images and fantasies improves their self-esteem, quality of life, and sense of social place.

In terms of the "literary merit" of the books, I am struck by their conventional narrative formats. Each story is motivated by the development of a first-person character. Usually he is a gay man with a particular job, sensibility, or environment who is motivated by psychological or emotional issues. Typically through his relationship with another man—an intense, personal relationship involving sex and often love, the protagonist resolves or moves beyond his initial interior conflict. John consistently used accepted literary structures of character and description recognized in every college classroom where writing is taught and analyzed.

These relationships are always presented in the context of the narrator's autobiography. In the story "Pedro," he recounts growing up in New England, hitchhiking as a boy as his first strategy for meeting other gay men. This places his work in a specific historic context because he was only able to experience his homosexuality through the anonymity of these seductions. Hopefully, a young man growing up in John's hometown today would have other ways of living his homosexuality if he wanted them. Some of those changes, that widening of choices and opportunities for gay teenagers, are a result of lifelong efforts by people like John Preston to bring these experiences out of isolation and into common knowledge. This is the context for the sexual description in John's work.

In "Pedro," John describes his first experience of being in love and in a couple. Pedro meets the narrator's parents and brings them gifts. John describes his own transformation from a bookish loner into a lover. And the sexuality between him and Pedro is completely relevant to the development of the story. It is part of his character's feelings of passion, desire, and satisfaction and underlines accurately the tension between his parents' homophobia and the joy of his sexuality with his lover.

In the story "An Education," John's protagonist has graduated from college, is working towards a graduate degree in sex counseling, and has come to a major city to attend a conference for sex therapy professionals. He goes from stuffy academic conference rooms to the more personally revealing atmosphere of men's bars. The hypocrisy of his professional position becomes increasingly obvious. Ultimately, through an intense sexual and psychological relationship with a man he meets in a bar, the protagonist is so changed that he is unable, at the close of the story, to resume his professional demeanor. The story is structured in such a way as to juxtapose the banal theoretical comments and cynical attitudes of the sex therapists with the protagonist's experience of his new sexual relationship as provocative, profoundly transforming, and deeply passionate.

The books are united further by the through-line of John's life. He is always referring to his daily routine in Maine, meeting friends for dinner, remembering incidents about his family, noticing his own ageing process. His work is rooted, always in the personal. In this way John's books have now become historical documents about rituals, language, sex acts, fashions in clothing and appearance that describe a sector of gay male life before the onset of the AIDS epidemic. Every interaction is set within a particular context reflective of that time. Whether it is Provincetown at its height or the Mineshaft before it was closed by the New York City Police Department, the seductions, the sex, the friendships are all particular to a disappeared era. This alone merits their preservation.

But even more important to this work is John's fascination with and devotion to men. He was willing to risk repression and isolation as a writer in order to honestly depict and express this depth of feeling. And by placing his own desires within the context of everyday life, John's books move towards a normalization of homosexual love and passion. Given the hostility surrounding his work, these actions were visionary, prophetic ones—based more in a freer future than in the emotionally denying real world in which he worked.

In the final chapter of *I Once Had a Master,* John discusses his own work in the context of contemporary political discourse on writing about sexuality and the body. The self-consciousness and ability to grasp intellectually complex social and aesthetic questions places this essay in the realm of literary theory. He reveals the meaning of his books to his larger community, the dialogue between himself and his readers about his work, the social context in which it appeared, and how he wished it to be viewed. These concerns make clear that John considered his work to be of literary merit and that, in fact, it was also viewed that way by his readers and publishers.

John Preston's depictions of sexual power dynamics between lovers do contain social commentary. While Pat Califia's depictions highlight women's social and political inequality and the role that sexual play can have in reinforcing a sense of equity, power, and self-esteem, John Preston's male characters refrain from the classic heroic male behavior codified in literature. They do not bully, violate, or conquer women, children, or other weaker men. Instead they bring their desires and abilities relating to sexual power purely into a consensual arena. These gay male characters can use their sexual imaginations to mitigate oppressive practices aimed at them from a prejudicial dominant culture. Given these dimensions to Preston's work, it is confusing to note that other books of more challenging sexual content such as the internationally recognized classic *The Story of O* by Pauline Réage and the Beauty Trilogy by Anne Rice are available in Canada while John's work was singled out for restriction.

The actual testifying did not go that well. Once I got on the witness stand, the Crown claimed that I was not qualified to be an expert on "harm." I said that as someone who has experienced "harm" for being a lesbian, and especially for being a lesbian writer, I was quite expert on the matter. I argued that "homophobia is a social pathology that causes violence and destroys families." I said that gay and lesbian books are a mitigating force against homophobia and therefore are socially beneficial and the opposite of "harm." The Crown claimed that I was not qualified to make this statement because I am not a sociologist. They won, and I was forbidden from addressing that issue in court.

This was the first indication I had of our judge's conceptual limits. As we moved along, I came to learn that Milord did not know what "deconstruction" meant. And later he revealed a puzzlement over the meaning of the word "enema." *Oh no,* I thought. *If he has never heard of enemas or deconstruction, we are doomed.*

The Crown read out loud a passage from one of John's books describing nipple torture. It was a bit surreal. Then he asked me if this was "degrading or dehumanizing." I did my best.

Through the rest of the trial the government repeatedly made clear their view about any gay sex. They had seized a lesbian anthology called *Bushfire* because it included the line "she held me tightly like a rope," which they said was "bondage." They had also seized a book called *Stroke*, which was about boating.

In the end, after many more years and courts and dollars, Little Sister lost their case. The judge ruled that Canada customs officials had, and still have, the right to decide which materials are not suitable to come into the country. Interestingly, they quickly ratified gay marriage, while continuing to retain the right to insure that no married gay man will ever go looking for *Mister Benson.*

Those two days in court made it crystal clear to me that in the minds of many people, homosexuality is inherently pornographic. And there is nothing that has occurred in the subsequent three presidential terms that has created any other kind of context. The best proof is in our contemporary placement and treatment of sexually truthful gay literature. That John

Preston was invited to give a keynote address at Outwrite, the now defunct lesbian and gay writers' conference, was a sign of the prominent and central role of sexually explicit content in gay literature when it was controlled by the community. Now that gay presses and bookstores have been gentrified out of existence, first by chain stores like Barnes and Nobles, which are now being outsold by Amazon.com, gay literature is at the mercy of the mainstream. Many of the male writers with primary gay content who are rewarded and accepted by the mainstream create characters that are inadvertently palatable to heterosexual liberals. We all love David Sedaris, but he doesn't write explicitly about his Master. Other, smarmier, highly rewarded works show gay men who are alone, betray each other, commit suicide, who have demure and coded sex. The few men who manage to get published at the highest levels with sexually true materials, like Edmund White, still remain on the outside of the straight literary power elite.

John Updike, in 1999 wrote a stunningly idiotic attack on Alan Hollinghurst's novel *The Spell* in which he accused Hollinghurst of being "relentlessly gay" and sexist because he is gay, and referring to the author's community of gay men as "a Genet prison without the guards." Updike wrote that only heterosexuals' lives involve the "perpetuation of the species and the ancient, sacralized structures of the family." Although many gay and lesbian writers including myself and Craig Lucas wrote letters of protest to the *New Yorker*, none were published. When Updike died, only gay novelist Karl Soehnlein even mentioned the incident, as the endless mainstream tributes were silent.

Barnes and Nobles makes the obscenity inherent in homosexuality explicit by pulling novelists with enough integrity to be out in their work, off of the fiction shelves, and hiding them in the gay and lesbian section, which is usually upstairs on the fourth floor behind the potted plants. Mainstream book awards agree by ignoring overtly lesbian fiction, as do mainstream review and publication venues. If the *New Yorker* has ever published a lesbian story by an out American lesbian writer, I've missed it. If Terry Gross has ever interviewed an out American lesbian novelist with a lesbian protagonist, I've missed it. If Charlie Rose has ever interviewed an out lesbian American novelist for a book with a lesbian protagonist, it has escaped me. If the *New York Review of Books* . . . et cetera, et cetera. They all agree that this work belongs behind the potted plants. If any multicharacter play inside an authorial universe (i.e., not performance art, vaudeville, or stand-up) with depth, authenticity, gravitas, and a lesbian protagonist has ever gotten more than one production in the United States of America, it eluded me. Television shows—beyond a handful of cable series—don't have sexual gay protagonists, commercial movies with explicit gay sex are few and far between. The only thing that seems to evict homosexual sex from the realm of the pornographic, in some people's minds, is marriage. Which reaffirms my argument, since nothing is more desexualizing than marriage. This puts gentrified gay people in a terrible bind: we can dissociate ourselves from the full continuum of queer literature, that is, from queer sexuality, thereby falsely describing our literature as "quality" if its sexual content is acceptable to straights. But that is a kind of implicit agreement that we only become deserving of rights when presenting as somewhere between furtive and monogamous.

Specifically regarding lesbian content, which Urvashi Vaid insightfully called "the Kiss of Death," is there any literature that has been as gentrified out of existence as fiction by American lesbian writers with lesbian protagonists? After the gentrification economy/value system killed so many small presses, bookstores, countercultural newspapers, magazines, gatherings, conversations, imaginings, and expressions, lesbian content fell upon the mercy of the replacement system and that system had no mercy. U.S. lesbian literature has endured a fifteen-year period of profound censorship in which most lesbian writers who have lesbian protagonists have been driven out of writing or abandoned their content in order to stay in print. The equation has been made brutally clear. If the work has a lesbian protagonist it is no good. It is badly written, meaningless, and undeserving of recognition. Ask people with power in the industry who is the greatest American lesbian writer. Their answer? Susan Sontag, who never applied her prodigious gifts to articulating her own condition. She even wrote a book analyzing AIDS stigma while staying in the content closet—as a result, it is the most cited book in AIDS literature, seen as more legitimate than those written by out queers. There are numbers of writers, filmmakers, historians, actors, directors who may not hide that they are lesbians, but would never assert their right to a protagonist as explicit about the author's own realities as every other writer is about theirs. If they were to do so, these gifted women would become second rate automatically. It kind of reminds me of Black movie actor Step'n Fetchit (real name: Lincoln Theodore Monroe Andrew Perry). At the very moment that Black people were doing a great deal of the hard labor of this country with no appropriate compensation, he earned millions by portraying a Black man who was, of all things, *lazy*. The very thing that Black men were not. For gifted lesbians, the greatest recognition awaits if they do pretend the opposite of the truth, if they replace the complex, human, fascinating details of their own experience/history with the pretense that

that experience is not worthy of mention. They must agree that we do not deserve to be protagonists.

When I was a child, the dominant culture could still pretend that lesbians did not exist except as predators. While of course modernism allowed for some women to be out to some degree in their work, and pulp fiction reserved a stigmatized place in popular reading culture, a full range of literary motifs with lesbian protagonists was only allowed to start to come to the surface in the 1970s. But this work, even the tip of the iceberg that was allowed to be seen in the most mainstream of places, was fueled by the passion, money, and attention of a mass political movement. Once that dissipated with Reaganism, AIDS, and gentrification, lesbian literature became more dependent on traditional modes of literary acknowledgement and support to exist.

A report published by the Astrea Foundation in 1999 documented how private funding was ignoring lesbian writers, and creating incentive for serious artists to avoid lesbian content. By 2009, we now see the consequences of the institutionalized underdevelopment they warned us about. The report stated that

> there are many stages of closetedness and openness in the current literary market, and they have distinct relationships to foundation support. In today's climate, lesbians who are closeted personally and in their creative work are the most likely to receive funding. Almost every foundation that we examined funded women in this category.
>
> The second most likely group for support were women who were openly lesbian or bisexual in the gay and lesbian media, but omit or deny their same-sex experiences in the mainstream media. None of these women had primary lesbian content in their work. They have had secondary characters, sub-plots, or coded or euphemistic content that could be read by a lesbian reader but they never represented their own homosexuality on the page in the way that

heterosexual writers currently represent their own feelings and experiences.

The third most likely group for support are women who are completely out personally, but are known to the dominant group for creative work with no primary lesbian content.

The final category, women who are out personally and in their work, are almost completely excluded from foundation support in fiction.

The Astrea study assessed board composition and the selection process. They found that while all foundations discriminated against work with openly lesbian content, they were equally divided on gay male content. When a foundation excluded gay male content, they did so completely. When they supported it, they did so systematically. Surprisingly, the study found no correlation between gender parity and gay funding. Foundations with conscientious gender parity in grant-giving often completely excluded openly gay and lesbian work.

The study uncovered that it was virtually impossible for openly lesbian work to be awarded on *internal nomination only* basis. The only American writer with primary lesbian content to get private funding in the entire decade, Blanche Boyd, was awarded a Guggenheim in fiction through an application-based process.

I want to reproduce for you here the granting patterns of the six major private supporters of fiction writing by openly gay and lesbian artists with out protagonists in the United States during the entirety of the 1990s.

1. The MacArthur Fellowship Program (internal nomination)

	MEN	WOMEN
1990	Guy Davenport	None
1991	None	None

1992	None	None
1993	None	None
1994	None	None
1995	None	None
1996	None	None
1997	None	None
1998	None	None
1999	None	None

2. The Guggenheim Fellowship Program in Fiction (application)

1990	None	None
1991	None	None
1992	Mathew Stadler	None
1993	Michael Cunningham	Blanche Boyd
1994	Randall Keenan, Dale Peck	None
1995	None	None
1996	None	None
1997	None	None
1998	None	None
1999	None	None

3. The Whiting Foundation Writers Program (internal nomination)

1990	None	None
1991	None	None
1992	Robert Jones	None
1993	None	None
1994	Randall Keenan	None
1995	Michael Cunningham, Mathew Stadler	None
1996	None	None
1997	Anderson Farrell	None

1998	None	None
1999	Not offered	Not offered

4. The Lila Wallace / Readers' Digest Fund (internal nomination)

1990	None	None
1991	None	None
1992	None	None
1993	None	None
1994	None	None
1995	None	None
1996	None	None
1997	None	None
1998	None	None
1999	Jim Grimsley	None

5. The Lannan Foundation (internal nomination)

1990	None	None
1991	None	None
1992	None	None
1993	None	None
1994	None	None
1995	None	None
1996	None	None
1997	None	None
1998	None	None
1999	None	None

6. The American Academy of Arts and Science (internal nomination)

1990	None	Jeanette Winterson
1991	Alan Holinghurst	None

1992	None	None
1993	James Purdy	None
1994	Daryl Pinckney	None
1995	Jim Grimsley	None
1996	Larry Kramer, Randall Keenan	None
1997	None	None
1998	None	None
1999	Jim Grimsley	None

The study concluded:

> In the current climate of conservatism and niche marketing, American literature with primary lesbian content is being increasingly marginalized. There are many factors contributing to this process including marketing aimed only at gay and lesbian readers, low advances, low sales expectations by publishers, quota systems in review venues, segregation in chain stores, exclusion from mainstream awards, and more.
>
> When such a significant force systematically withholds support from lesbian literature, there are concrete results. Most importantly, lesbian writers are pressured to drop the lesbian content from their work in order to earn a living, win prestige and recognition, and thereby win good teaching jobs and have cultural influence. Not only will this silence writers without independent means, but it will dissuade younger writers from being out in their work.

By 2009, these predictions became reality. Today if you are a lesbian and want to get married in Iowa, you are in luck. But if you are a human being who would like to read novels with lesbian protagonists by openly lesbian authors, close your eyes and think of England. In the United Kingdom, right now, openly lesbian writers with lesbian content like Jeanette Winterson and Sarah Waters are treated like people and their books are treated like books. They are published by the most mainstream publishers, are represented by high-rolling agents, are reviewed in regular newspapers by real critics, contextualized with other British intellectuals, given mainstream awards, have their stories broadcast on television and as a result of all this respect and consideration, they are read by a broad constituency in England and the rest of the world.

For those of us writing here in the gentrified United States, England seems like the promised land. Here, lesbian literature has gone the way of cheap rents, good public schools, nonmonogamy, integrated neighborhoods, and free will. At the 2008 Lambda Literary Awards (the awards the LGBT community gives to books ignored by straight book awards) not a single lesbian book nominated for best novel was published by a mainstream press. Our literature is disappearing at the same time that we are being told we are winning our rights. How can we be equal citizens if our stories are not allowed to be part of our nation's story?

So, gay men's literature and lesbian literature have been impacted on and transformed by gentrification in profoundly different ways. Gay men have learned to eradicate their sexuality, their anger, and their experiences of heterosexual cruelty in order to be invited into the category of "literature." And then they have forgotten that this is different than what they produced before what we should only sarcastically and ironically call "acceptance." Lesbian literature has been gentrified out of existence, through a systematic series of punishments and critical exclusions that now make its production unimaginable for artists working seriously who want to be recognized.

Of course, I am ever the optimist and wonder if the collapse of behemoth publishing can help us poke back through the fog, back into the intellectual life of our own country. This year I am on the jury of two queer book prizes, and so have a chance to read every lesbian book published in North American in 2010. Some are pretty good. My favorites include *Sub Rosa* by Amber Dawn, published by Arsenal Pulp Press—a moody atmospheric novel about a young street prostitute in Canada who barely knows what she is doing/experiencing/feeling. The author conveys the story in a gorgeously stylized replication of the protagonist's consciousness—we see it all through her fog, and thereby understand with even more depth what her true story is. Or Eileen Myles's *Inferno*, published by O Books, in which this energetic, funny, formally engaged, almost mythic writer—who has inspired two generations of lesbian literature—somehow brings together her own story, Dante, and a social history of the New York School by the natural propulsion of her own charm on the page. Out of the sixty-something books I looked at, only two had mainstream publishers. Most importantly, neither of those had openly lesbian editors. Therein lies the problem. The most truthful, moving, and advanced works we are producing are being ignored by the women who can be out in their jobs today, because of the work of fearless out lesbians of the past and present. The editors are gentrified, they don't understand their own responsibilities. It's all a blur, translating into a problematic lack of consciousness and a low level of ambition. Not that it is only the editors' responsibility, absolutely not. But when you look at the thousands of boring books by straight people that not only have nothing to offer, but financially tank—why should our most interesting writers be constantly sent to Siberia? Punished for telling the truth and writing well? And yet we persevere, that's what is so exciting. You can't kill lesbian literature—even if the authors are driven insane and into silence one by one, there is always someone else willing to carry on the fight. The impulse to express and understand will always compel some people with integrity. And integrity has its own strange trajectory—greater than any one person. Now that is a good lesson of history.

Degentrification

The Pleasure of Being Uncomfortable

> Happiness for some involves persecution for others;
> it is not simply that this happiness produces a social
> wrong, but it might even be dependant upon it.
>
> Sara Ahmed, *Queer Phenomenology*

As a nation we have long understood the conformity of the 1950s partially as a consequence of the trauma of World War II. Our young men signed up and were drafted out of their provincial towns and neighborhoods and witnessed/experienced/committed large-scale violence. They came home wanting stability of status, a known world. Back in the United States, veterans were offered the G.I. bill. Now they could go to college for free and get low-interest loans on suburban homes. While these significant advantages allowed many men to move from the working to the middle class and beyond, it also gave them a huge, sudden leap over women in educational level and financial power.

Women, who had experienced more economic autonomy and agency during the war, were now repositioned back into a submissive role. People of color and gay people who had fought in Europe and the Pacific returned to Jim Crow and compulsory heterosexuality. Internationally, McCarthyism (and the postwar imperialism it justified) strongly reinforced the United States in reactionary capitalism, where the market interdependence with familial privatization made citizenship more complicit with excess and consumerism. The sexual and gender progress, the racial striving of the 1920s and 1930s, the benefits of social programs like WPA became the past, as America was repositioned into 1950s suburban culture—a racially segregated, class-stratified, highly gendered closed system. Over time this system proved unbearable; fifteen years later it exploded into revolutionary thinking, sexual liberation, and mass movements for social change.

It seems to me that gay people are currently undergoing a similar path. The trauma of AIDS—a trauma that has yet to be defined or understood, for which no one has been made accountable—has produced a gentrification of the mind for gay people. We have been streamlining into a highly gendered, privatized family/marriage structure en masse.

What have we internalized as a consequence of the AIDS crisis? As with most historical traumas of abuse, the perpetrators—the state, our families, the media, private industry—have generally pretended that the murder and cultural destruction of AIDS, created by their neglect, never actually took place. They pretend that there was nothing they could have done, and that no survivors or witnesses are walking around today with anything to resolve. They probably believe, as they are pretending, that the loss of those individuals has had no impact on our society, and that the abandonment and subsequent alienation of a people and culture does not matter. But of course, that could not be farther from the truth. My own study of the AIDS activist movement, the ACT UP Oral History Project, reveals the true message of AIDS,

> that a despised group of people with no rights or representation, who were
> abandoned by their government, families, and society, facing a terminal
> illness, bonded together against great odds and forced this culture—
> *against its will*—to change its behavior towards people with AIDS, thereby
> saving each other's lives.

This is the most remarkable story I have ever experienced, and it should be and *could* be a model for human behavior in all realms. The true message of the AIDS crisis is that making people with power accountable works. This message, however, is obscured and unavailable (temporarily, we hope), not known by many people gay or straight. Instead, what most people internalize, falsely, as the dominant message of the AIDS crisis is that (1) our sexuality is dangerous and should be contained; and (2) no one cares what happens to us.

In this way, gay people are the new Jews. So traumatized by mass death and the indifference of others, we assimilate into the culture that allowed us to be destroyed. We access their values and use them to *replace* our own in a way that undermines our distinction and strength. In this process, we can take on oppressive roles—for example the increasing anti-immigrant sentiments of assimilated LGB people in Europe, or pro-military attitudes accompanying the Don't Ask, Don't Tell repeal.

For lesbians, the parallels to the fifties are even starker. The LGBT community is a community of men and woman/males and females, and people who don't identify with the binary gender system. We don't, for the most part, reproductively mate for reasons of romantic love and sexual desire—but nonetheless there is a dynamic interrelationship of sympathies, bonds and contradictions and conflicts. During the AIDS crisis, the sexist imbalance of the gay community was overwhelmed by the necessities of trauma. Men became endangered and vulnerable. They needed each other and women to intervene with the government, media, and pharmaceutical and insurance industries. They needed intervention in all arenas of social relationship. They needed women's political experience from the earlier feminist and lesbian movements, women's analysis of power, and women's emotional commitments to them. They needed women's alienation from the state. As men became weak, they allowed themselves to acknowledge the real ways that women are strong, particularly recognizing our hard-won experience at political organizing. There was more room for women to be seen at our level of merit, to occupy social space that we deserved to occupy, even if the reason was that men were disappearing. Like Rosie the Riveter, gay women gained more equality within the queer community, more social currency and autonomy because men were threatened, wounded, and killed.

As protease inhibitors normalized AIDS, this relationship shifted back. Men began to regain their collective health and with that their patriarchal imperatives. Male power returned with t-cells and lesbians occupied a much more ambiguous and unstable social role. I often think about this when I am operating inside the white patriarchy called the American theater. White gay men have an open and explicit level of power in the theater that they don't experience in many other realms.

They are vicious in their disrespect of non-gay-icon-type women's perspectives and their favoritism towards other men. There is a level of sexist corruption so blatant, it merits them losing all their federal, state, and city funding for violation of nondiscrimination policies. As I experience regular diminishing, cruel, or stupid behavior from some sexist gay man in the theater, I often think about how the fact that he is alive—whether HIV-positive or -negative—is in part a consequence of my own actions and the actions of many women he knows and will never know. But now that that history is invisible, *these* men—once vulnerable—now again feel superior. Now that *we* need *them* to let *us* into the power system of representation that they control, there is no reciprocity. This is depressing and also defeating. I can understand why gay women of my generation retreat from the community relationship, like their 1950s foremothers, into the highly gendered but recognizably legitimate social role of lesbian mother.

Everyone wants to be a good parent, and LGBT parents have to make deliberate, elongated efforts to get their children. The obstacles to insemination and adoption require a strong need to parent. Unfortunately, in our real world, large numbers of children grow up to be victims, perpetrators, or bystanders. Very few children actually grow up to make the world a better place. Personally, I don't feel that creating new victims, perpetrators, and bystanders is the great social ooh-and-aah that it is made out to be. I do understand that people want to have children for reasons personal to their own needs, not necessarily for the child or for the world, and perhaps that's reason enough, but I don't know why.

Observing my very decent friends raise their children is—of course—a fascinating experience. Many of these children have the same anger, sadness, cruelty, passivity, neediness and narcissism, and the same unfulfilled potential as most adults I know. I see the future.

Being a great parent is so tough—it requires that the parent feel loved and accepted enough themselves that they don't need to control or construct another person, while still being able to be disciplined and provide structure, love, security, and guidance. Having children to end loneliness, to win parental approval, to feel normal, to heal past traumas may all be fine for the parent, but does it work for the child and the community? Sometimes. Most of my kind, loving, well-intentioned friends are human and therefore problematic parents, like all parents. They project onto their kids, which is normal. They threaten, make false "deals," give false information, are arbitrary with boundaries, indulge excessively in objects. Some of them are in relationships that are not dynamic, truly loving, or sexual. More families-by-habit and fear of being alone, more displaced unhappiness and emotional control or neglect of their kids. More brilliant women unable to make larger contributions because they are parenting a sad, spoiled, frightened, complicit, or bullying child. Since these parents are too busy and overwhelmed in the domestic sphere to champion collective child care, for example, the rest of us lose as well. We lose access to our friends, their gifts/skills/ideas, we lose their presence. We have to cover for them or submit to them when they have child care needs. Even at work, we—the unparenting—are supposed to privilege our colleagues' needs for child care, compensate for the lack of governmental responsibility. After so many years of radical thinking, creating new paradigms and working collectively to end the AIDS crisis, fight for economic autonomy and social justice, create new representations—after all that awareness and action,

I often see my most brilliant female friends reduced to endless conversations about private school. If they wanted me to join them in creating movements for radical child care reforms of course I would. But I don't see much leadership coming directly from that overwhelmed corner. Yet. I still have hope.

I'm an optimist and believe that this period of conformity is in part a reflection of the conservative tenor of our nation as a whole, and in part an unacknowledged consequence of AIDS trauma. And that it can't last forever. So, pressure to marry and have children, institutionalized monogamy, social recognition through marriage and motherhood, financially strapped female parents, relationships by habit, sexual repression, the propensity of single parent lesbian households due to lack of accountability, identity by consumerism, privatized living, lack of community, over-burdened projecting broke parents, obstacles to being productive . . . sound familiar? Can the Gay Fifties last forever? Thankfully not. Just as with straight people, these 1950s values of control and homogeneity will probably prove to be unbearable at some point and we will have a swing back in the other direction towards LGBT communal living, sexual revolutions, and collectivity. I hope I live long enough to see my prediction come to pass.

In the 1930s, European psychiatrist Wilhelm Reich started a movement in Germany that he called "Sex-Pol," thereby coining the phrase later popularized by Kate Millet, "sexual politics." Sex-Pol attempted to combine Communist and psychoanalytic thinking about sexuality. Reich would go to working-class people and say, "You know why your sex lives are so lousy? It's because you don't have decent housing conditions. You have to sleep in the same bed as your children and can't express yourselves freely. Fight for housing reforms so that you can have a better sex life."

Now, of course, because this was brilliant and true, he ended up getting thrown out of both the German Communist Party and the Psychoanalytic League. The Communists didn't like sex and the shrinks didn't like Communists, and were busy trying to appease the Nazis. However, his ideas spoke to large numbers and at one point forty to fifty thousand people were involved in Sex-Pol. I think it is inevitable that LGBT people will come around to this kind of integration again, a melding of the human need for free sexual expression with a sense of social justice—the combination that was at the heart of gay liberation, lesbian nation, and AIDS activism. So, if this is our "1954" and nothing great is going to happen until "1966," we're back in the prerevolutionary days—when so much newly preliminary and yet foundational work can be done.

As in the mid-twentieth century, one of the things we need to work out for ourselves is a true definition of happiness. Are we being duped by gentrified happiness, and can we find pleasure in something more complex, more multi-dimensional, and therefore more dynamic? Can we be happy with the uncomfortable awareness that other people are real?

Gentrification replaces most people's experiences with the perceptions of the privileged and calls that reality. In this way gentrification is dependant on telling us that things are better than they are—and this is supposed to make us feel happy. It's a strange concept of happiness as something that requires the denial of many other people's experiences. For some of us, on the other hand, the pursuit of reality is essential to happiness. Even if the process gets us in trouble. It is very hard to get a glimpse of what is actually happening when one is constantly being lied to, and it is even harder to articulate what we realize is actually happening while intuiting that punishment awaits.

One thing I have learned over and over again is that asking people with false power to be accountable makes them very very angry. It makes them vicious. In the case of women intellectuals, mockery and dismissal are the easiest modes of punishment—but the range of strategies of diminishment is very broad. It's frightening to have ideas that are alienating. I've certainly had moments where I suddenly crack the deception and *get* what is really going on, and then . . . *oh shit*, I understand that this information is not going to be peacefully received.

· · ·

> The healthy, conceited female wants the company
> of equals whom she can respect and groove on.
> (Valerie Solanas)

We're repeatedly told that women are thriving in our society. More women than men are in college, we see women in male professions, as powerful figures on television, and as consumers. Yet at the same time that women apparently have broken all barriers, a disobedient female is considered antisocial, a drag, and a bitch. Although feminism succeeded in transforming options and ways of thinking, the subsequent changes have remained encased in the capitalist apparatus. At the same time, our propaganda machine, mass entertainment, has erased the history of feminism and how these changes were actually achieved. So only their consequences remain visible. Because there has never been a major play, or smash hit movie or musical, or widely read best-selling book about women's rights—no *Angels in America*, no *Roots*, no *And the Band Played On*, no *Autobiography of Malcolm X*, no *Milk*—most Americans have no idea of how women organized or won anything, while knowing everything about baseball, Lady Gaga, and eating in Provence.

As Ti-Grace Atkinson articulated at the fortieth anniversary of the Columbia University student rebellion, women can only progress in a progressive era. Women cannot advance unless men are also advancing. And this occurs every thirty to forty years. The interim periods are years of giveback. While some individuals consecrate their lives to trying to protect earlier wins, they pay an enormous personal price for being so against the reactionary current. In our era, these protectors have managed to retain some crucial lasting reforms of feminism including:

- Increased education for women
- Mechanisms for state intervention into domestic violence and child abuse
- Continuing legality of birth control and abortion, although access to abortion is severely compromised

What has not changed much are:

- Attitudes about women's inferiority to men
- Access to power
- Earning capacity
- Lack of accurate representation in our media culture
- Participation in the creation of culture, policy, and point of view
- Emotional responsibilities in parenting and partnering
- Lesbians are still treated as irrelevant nonpersons

Despite the gentrified feeling that women now have what we need, the reality is that American women have not gained access to the wealth of the nation and do not have control over the perspectives by which national cultural decisions are made. Yet we are told that women are now basically equal. The current foreclosure crisis is disproportionately affecting women because of our lack of economic power, but is not described that way in the press. The increasingly common use of wealth to exploit people who do not have wealth through immoral lending practices, like high interest credit cards, subprime mortgages, debt acquisition through lack of medical coverage, et cetera, affects women in significantly larger numbers than men. In short, capitalism, which is currently administering the gains women have made, is increasingly a system of men denying money to or taking money from women. So what is really happening is available just under the surface of the false story.

Acting in a way that acknowledges that our structures are not neutral or natural is a tough assignment. Mysteriously, and yet humanly, progressive periods are determined by the zeitgeist. When they happen it is undeniable and you can't force it. But in the meantime it is important to keep rigorous thought and small, accountable action alive. Of course is it not always possible to behave in recognition of the true nature of our structures—how they create supremacy ideology and pretend it is real—because the punishment is too severe. But the hope is that a critical mass of us can be more aware and vocal enough to threaten gentrified thinking without actually hurting ourselves. We want to be what Judy Grahn called "the flea in the elephant's nose" without getting trampled. Revolutionary thinking means focusing on the frame, rather than on the goodies within it, but reality means doing this to the extent that you can without being victimized by the folks who don't want to be accountable.

In preparing this book, I reread Emma Goldman's *My Further Disillusionment in Russia*—it is incredibly relevant. She very humanely reveals how she arrived in Russia as a political deportee from the United States, committed to the ideals of the very recent revolution. With great self-criticism and a really clear communication of her process, she shows how she learned to identify Soviet supremacy ideology and what happened when she tried to make its perpetrators accountable. There are even great cameos with Gorki, Kropotkin, and Lenin himself! The consequence, of course, was that she was redeported back to America. Both America and Russia "didn't want to talk about it," the "it" being accountability. In the documentary film *Anarchism In America* this is a small piece of sync-sound newsreel footage of Goldman arriving back in the port of New York, with no passport. She has to be very careful if she is to stay in America.

"Miss Goldman," a reporter asks. "What is the difference between the United States of America and the Soviet Union?"

With her thick Jewish accent, and absolute bespectacled deadpan, she carefully replies. "The United States of America and the Soviet Union are the two most interesting countries in the world."

Needless to say, she was deported to Canada where she died penniless.

Her devotion to the pursuit of justice blinded her from fully understanding the brutality of her enemies, and she ended up crushed. Like many before her and since, she grossly underestimated the cruelty of her opponents, because it was unimaginable to someone like her. She couldn't understand a person going that far to not have to question themselves. While she experienced joy in discovery and truth, the punishment she received resulted in a lost opportunity for happiness that her excess suffering created. Which leads us to the not small question of happiness. What it is, how to tell the truth and still have it, and the necessity of experiencing happiness without doing so at other people's expense are questions we have to grapple with.

Gentrified happiness is often available to us in return for collusion with injustice. We go along with it, usually, because of the privilege of dominance, which is the privilege not to notice how our way of living affects less powerful people. Sometimes we do know that certain happiness exists at the expense of other human beings, but because we're not as smart as we think we are, we decide that this is the only way we can survive. Stupidity or cruelty become the choice, but it doesn't always have to be that way. After all, people and institutions act on and transform each other. So, it's not happiness at the expense of the weaker versus nothing, right? And yet we are led to feel this way.

Depending on our caste and context, opportunities are regularly presented that enable us to achieve more safety by exploiting unjust systems. Whether we are benefiting from globalization, U.S. markets, or being able to get a job/apartment, a play production, or a relationship because of prejudicial structures that give us unfair advantages as Americans or whites or educated people, or people with homes or people with running water or people with health insurance, or people who can afford to shop at Whole Foods, or whatever. We get to feel better precisely because someone else doesn't have what they need.

Conveniently there is a billion dollar self-help industry that tells us to treat the very skewed frame as if it were neutral: Accept it. Be grateful for it. Do not resist. This, we're told, will bring us more happiness. "Let go/Move on/Get over it." If you are the demographic that the frame was designed to inflate, accepting it will help you maximize its privileges. But if you are the demographic that the frame was designed to defeat or marginalize, accepting it makes it more effective for its intended beneficiaries. I think it is safe to say that personal happiness at the expense of other people's deprivation is a normative standard of gentrification culture, which depends on it to thrive.

This kind of conundrum is permitted by a cultural idea of happiness as something that requires absolute comfort. In order to transform the structures, we who benefit from them would have to accept that our privileges are enforced, not earned. And that others, who are currently created as inferior, just simply lack the lifelong process of false inflation and its concrete material consequence. Facing this would mean altering our sense of self from *deservingly superior* to *inflated*. That would be uncomfortable.

Herein lies the problem. We live with an idea of happiness that is based in other people's diminishment. But we do not address this because we hold an idea of happiness that precludes being uncomfortable. Being uncomfortable is required in order to be accountable. Be we currently live with a stupefying cultural value that makes being uncomfortable something to be avoided at all costs. Even at the cost of living a false life at the expense of others in an unjust society. We have a concept of happiness that excludes asking uncomfortable questions and saying things that are true but which might make us and others uncomfortable. Being uncomfortable or asking others to be uncomfortable is practically considered antisocial because the revelation of truth is tremendously dangerous to supremacy. As a result, we have a society in which the happiness of the privileged is based on never starting the process towards becoming accountable. If we want to transform the way we live, we will have to reposition being uncomfortable as a part of life, as part of the process of being a full human being, and as a personal responsibility.

Once we can embrace the fact that it won't kill us, and start the process, with repetition it becomes more tolerable. And once the prohibition on being uncomfortable is diluted, dismantling gentrified thinking and supremacy ideology becomes an interesting and natural part of being alive. Ultimately it becomes invigorating and then, exciting—I love the moment of recognition that I am uncomfortable and the process of trying to understand why. This insight makes my interior life richer, and I feel deeper and more human.

In my own world, I see these structures take place daily. I achieve happiness by having a secure job (tenure) with prestige (professor) and health insurance (GHI). At work I have the opportunity to share my gifts with a wide range of people (public university) and potentially see others benefit. My students treat me with a great deal of respect. I see some of them grow as a consequence of our relationship. I also see myself let down and obstruct students, and allow them to slip between the cracks, but even when I do this I do not get fired and do not lose my ability to go to the doctor. It would be impossible for me to be happy without medical insurance or a safe place to live. For now, this job helps me have those things—without it, I would not have them. Of course, there are other things that I need that this job will never give me: an elevator, a safe old age, long term care insurance. Maybe a car. Even for a city employee with a financially secure job, getting the elevator and the car in this economy usually requires having family money or a partner with a much higher income—it requires being floated in some way. When that is the case, the knowledge of the possibility of retirement contributes to happiness.

Spiritually, being a teacher is being a do-gooder. I am not a weapons manufacturer, a worker in genetic engineering agribusiness, or a cultural gatekeeper demeaning and depressing women artists on a daily basis. I don't market Fiji Water. Being at a public institution, while rough on many levels, also saves me from the task of being a tutor to the ruling class. Emotionally, I get the self-esteem that comes from being functional in a competitive system. Whenever we have a job opening at my school I see the hundreds of applicants desperate for income. Each one of my colleagues knows that they were able to get a job while many other competitors were not. It would be easy for me to tell myself that I am doing something positive with my life and ignore the contradictions.

Yet, if you really examine my employment situation, other structures become revealed. I work within a profoundly unjust paradigm, U.S. higher education, in which the quality of a person's education/diploma is determined principally by their class. Most of my students do not know how things work. They have no idea of how prestigious private universities function, what their conditions are, and how people who are produced by them think about themselves. They have delusions and misinformation about how people get rich, get power over their own lives, and make their dreams come true. They often don't understand how those dreams are constructed. They don't understand the actual process by which people become financially secure. Many of my students are the first in their families to go to college, are low income, are immigrants, and/or went to lousy public schools where they were not individuated. I can't tell you how often I get an email from a student that starts out, "Dear Professor Schulman, I am Nicole Santiago from your Tuesday Fiction Class." I always write back, "Nicole, I know who you are." The expectation that their teacher does not remember them, even after intimate direct conversations in class about their lives and work, is endemic. Many of my students make huge personal sacrifices to go to school. They take night classes, take out loans they cannot pay back, exhaust themselves with jobs, child care, and other responsibilities. They join the military. Many of our students do not own computers. Our school facilities are so poor that night school students do not have access to the writing center or child care, and we only have one truly functional smart classroom with projection capacity on the entire campus. The tiles are ripped, the classrooms are dirty, there is no centralized advisement office, so many students have no idea of what classes they are supposed to take. Required classes are not offered, are too large, and fill up quickly. I know for a fact that many of my students will not be able to fulfill their goals: home ownership, safe old age, lifelong appropriate insurance. They believe that making the above sacrifices will earn them these results, but in many cases it will not. The economic system of the United States is not designed to offer those levels of reward to most people, regardless of how hard they work.

As a teacher I am performing the nurturing role of person-building that is the stage set for public education. But simultaneously, while trying to impart the fundamentals of the craft of writing along with the fundamentals of critical thinking, I am also pretending to them that this degree will help them reach their goals. "Education is liberation" we discuss in Freshman Comp while reading *The Autobiography of Frederick Douglass.* "You've made a commitment to education," I say encouragingly. "So you understand that simple answers to complex questions rarely approach reality." There is a suggestive, cheerleading quality to my encouragements about reading, thinking, writing, analyzing. "I know that surpassing your family can be painful," I drop casually, knowing that some of my students have to justify their education to their families.

What I do not discuss with them that this degree in this school under these conditions and this level of class segregation is normalizing and pacifying them into the U.S. class system. I don't talk about how tenured professors like myself literally live off the backs of adjuncts in a feudally constructed system of privilege akin to the military in its fetishization of hierarchy. I do discuss the U.S. class system, and encourage students to look for answers in the reality of their own experiences instead of what they are told on television. But their realistic positionality in that system, and how little this degree will help them leave it, is not on my syllabus. It's a thin line between helping them move towards being informed versus depressing or humiliating them at what they are being kept from. Ultimately, I "do my job." I maintain the illusion of democracy so that a certain comfort level can be maintained in my relationship with my students, my relationship with my job, and their relationship with their college education. Although a handful do get to graduate school through enormous investment by the faculty, and we can and do help another handful get sophisticating experiences, in the end I get the emotional currency of being told by my students that I have "helped" them, when really I have participated in keeping them in their place.

Anything that humans construct, humans can transform. Other people can change you, why can't you change them? I can easily imagine a postgentrification era, where the critical mass that controls my school (teachers, administration, students) would decide that a fundamental part of our education should be to reveal the class structure truthfully. When we accept that this fact is an essential part of education, then these conversations in my classrooms would have a context, some kind of constructive goal, not just a burden dumped in the laps of hard-working but powerless students. I would love to trade—send our students to take one class each at Columbia and have each of their students come for one class with us. Just the difference of what is available in the cafeteria would be shocking. Just comparing the libraries would be shocking. Just comparing the classroom technology capacities would be illuminating. We could construct our whole university program around revealing to our students the realities of how things work, who designs them, who they are designed to serve, and the ever-important *feeling* of being privileged.

In the meantime, I do take risks to address a wide range of frameworks of power and replacement, gentrification and supremacy ideology. I do it enough to cause some trouble for myself, but mostly with institutions who would completely exclude me if I didn't speak up, even though they pretend that I've caused the exclusion by being "a bitch." I don't do it enough to get completely ejected, unless I underestimate dramatically the cowardice and brutality of the power I am addressing. In those cases I get crushed. When I came out as a lesbian and decided to be truthful and out in my work, I lost a lot, which does reduce my happiness. I have to meet a higher bar in all arenas. Because of my character, I am willing to experience a continued diminishment of stature and access, a loss of safety and currency and a disdain of the powerful as a consequence of being truthful in my work. But this causes me enormous pain and anxiety which also reduces my happiness. But, simultaneously, I am willing to be uncomfortable if that's what it takes to understand what is actually going on. Insight increases my happiness. I feel happy having a sense of intellectual integrity and integrity of action. I need to feel aware to feel content. I enjoy understanding things. Being willing to be uncomfortable in order to strive towards accountability brings me inner strength, which is a source of happiness. I love discovery. It's fun. I need a sense of decency towards and from others in order to be happy. I feel happiness when I figure out what is really going on. However, if in the end my search for what is real results in so much marginalization that I will not have a safe old age, then I will not be happy. Time will tell.

In the meantime, I'm excited to see what will happen next.

July 8, 2009—I read two interesting and relevant pieces in the news. The *New York Times* reports that speculators in Harlem are having trouble selling their wares. White developers who bought a series of brownstones on West 134th Street can't unload them. The cost of appropriate renovation is too high and the white gentry who were snapping up Harlem brownstones just don't have the cash. A companion piece on NPR reports that while housing prices are going up slightly, foreclosure rates are also increasing. This news reinforces my belief that the expansionism of gentrification has come to an end in New York City in our era.

But at the same time that I am taking this in, reading this article on-line and listening to NPR on-line, I am sitting in a hotel room in Suzhou, China where I have spent the last few weeks in my capacity as a college professor on an "educators' tour" of China. It did not take long for me to perceive that gentrification, the replacement of dynamic urban communities with homogeneity, is a wild elephant rampaging through the streets of eastern China much as it has in the East Village. Michael Meyer's superb and humane book *The Last Days of Old Beijing* documents the gentrification of Beijing in preparation for the 2008 Olympics. He describes the *hutong*, winding small-scale courtyard complexes—communities of neighbors who know everything about each other and share food, information, and toilets. As part of modernization, the Beijing government ordered these communities destroyed and their inhabitants resettled. In their place are modern high rises, highways, privatized housing, projects.

Meyer's description of life in his *hutong* reminds me of life in my building on Ninth Street, where I have lived since 1979. There are still about ten of us who have lived together as neighbors for twenty-five to thirty years. We have witnessed every relationship each other has had. We've watched each other through drug addiction, childbirth, changing sexual orientation, success, failure, screaming fights, financial disaster, EST, death, marriage, mental illness, joy. We had a successful rent strike for four years. We've united to save the apartments of two helpless tenants. The first was a shell-shocked Ukrainian World War II veteran whom the landlord tried to evict when his mother died. Willie Utkowitz thanked us with a case of Budweiser bought on his disability check. The second was a mentally ill, old-style butch lesbian who was born in the building and has spent the last twenty-five years barely getting by on methadone. None of the postgentrification neighbors have entered this relationship. Even the ones who have been here for fifteen years. The only times I hear from them are when faulty plumbing leaks into their apartment from mine and they get "angry." Or if I run into them at the gym. When they first move in, I try to be friendly—I introduce myself, invite them in for a chat—but it's never reciprocated. So the old timers exist in a community—gathering together annually for a solstice party. We are: me (a writer/teacher), Bill and Maria (a union cameraman/DP and his painter girlfriend), Lisa and Marta (an American/Polish lesbian couple with a teenage son who run a bookkeeping business), Sydelle (a retired school secretary). And we stay in touch with our old neighbors who have since moved out: Sarah (a social worker) and Steve and Monica (bakers). The other day I asked a new tenant what she does for a living. "I'm in branding," the thirty-something said, smiling.

In China, the *hutong* are being replaced in two distinctly different ways. When I was in Shanghai the city was in a turmoil of round-the-clock construction preparing for its celebration in 2010. *Hutong*, old neighborhoods, and human scale housing are being bulldozed and replaced with seventy-five-story buildings. You can drive on the thruway for forty-five minutes and never exit a sea of forty- to seventy-story apartment buildings housing Shanghai's twenty million inhabitants. So Chinese are being moved from neighborhoods where they knew everyone to gigantic buildings where they may never even know everyone on their floor. But there is another force after the *hutongs*—yuppies. The last ten years have produced the first crop of rich Chinese, and the entrepreneurial wild west environment is highly dynamic. Even though their businesses are theoretically taxed under socialism, actually—as in America—some elite businessmen don't pay taxes, so they have a lot of money, most of which is reinvested in their businesses. The government knows what is going on, but lets it happen as the extra cash makes economic development more dramatic. But the kinds of rich people being produced in China strangely replicate Western paradigms. On one hand there are the yuppies—they buy *hutong* and renovate them into luxury housing. When my friend Ismene, a German marketing executive, generously showed me the international businesswoman's side of Shanghai, I spent a great night talking and drinking white wine under the rarely seen Chinese moon on the roof terrace of her fully renovated rented *hutong* triplex. Stumbling home at 2 A.M., we passed her unrenovated neighbors, a family living behind a tailor shop in the place next door. Yuppie Chinese gentrify in classical style. Not only do they evict the poor, renovate their old buildings, and replace, but in Shanghai at least, they like to go out for martinis and Cold Stone Creamery ice cream in an upscale mall called Xintiandi, where identical pan-Asian designed expensive restaurants that could be found in any major city in America are filled with Chinese and foreigners in identical expensive clothing.

The other kind of Chinese gentrification was evident here in Suzhou where I had the great experience of meeting a Mr. Yee, an enterprising, interesting businessman who is part of a manufacturing business that has a thirty million dollar contract with Ikea. Yee believes that China will only get stronger and therefore invests in Chinese currency, not dollars, convinced that the yuan will gain in value. Yee kindly invited us to his "weekend" house outside of Suzhou. It was like a scene out of a Philip Roth novel. To escape from the crowded city—and Chinese people are almost never in quiet private places—his family bought a tract house in a luxury gated suburb. The kind of suburb that an American would buy a weekend house to get away from— antiseptic, new, and identical to that of his neighbors. Yee paid $150,000 four years ago (six years into his wealth) and claims that it is now worth $450,000, but a quick walk around the heavily guarded complex revealed that most of the cookie cutter houses were empty. He now plays golf at the adjacent course, a habit rich Chinese have recently acquired from the Japanese. His house is furnished around the plasma TV. The living room is filled with a collection of artificial stuffed dogs, and velour pillows in a faux Hopi pattern in Arizona earth colors. These pillows, I learn, are what his factory produces for Ikea—and I realize that they are sitting in identical suburban houses in New Jersey and Long Island.

A smart, interesting, and creative man, Yee sat with us in a teahouse and talked about the future of China. I asked him what he thought people could do with their money *after* they get their house, car, TV et cetera. He said he was asking himself the same question. It became apparent from our conversation that there is no culture of wealth in China. All rich are nouveau riche. And since the rich have only been that way for a decade or less, they have no sense of stable identity or confidence that their luck will continue. So they reinvest their money and buy schlock and kitsch for their homes. This led to a fascinating conversation about "power." In China, "power" is something that belongs to the central government. It's not associated with money, because the link between money and governmental policy has yet to be born. Business doesn't determine policy. The government doesn't ask them, Yee says. There is no conversation and no negotiation. Everything in China is top down. The idea that the rich could influence the culture of China through what they buy—for example if they bought paintings instead of stuffed dogs—is not yet under consideration. So there is a kind of gentrification without taste that is expressing itself in homogeneity.

Experiencing this made me wonder about the emotional attraction of gentrification. It's weirdly passive to commit gentrification, even though the consequence is brutal. It feels safe to be like others, and frightening to be one's self—because that requires knowing what one's true self is—and not in a New

Agey sense where anything one "feels" (a euphemism for wants) is right. But in a truthful sense, to see one's dark side and conflicts and in that way, realize one's self as human. Not as an excuse to not change, but as a starting point for change. But the future of Chinese gentrification was personified for us by the son of one of Mr. Yee's friends. A young, spoiled, lost child of privilege who had already dropped out of four American schools including Tacoma Lutheran College (one of those institutions that fulfill the Chinese wish for an American degree, any American degree). Bringing everything full circle, we went for a walk around his complex and I asked him what he wanted to do with his life. He told me he wants to live in a loft in one of his father's buildings and play pool and do "art stuff." Where did he get that paradigm from? It sounds so East Village.

In Michael Meyer's book he quotes an unnamed French architect working in Beijing. After years of experience he told Meyer, "The key to restoring buildings is to keep the original people inside."

Yes, the people are the heartbeat of the building. But, I can attest that the building is also the heartbeat of the tenant. Even more poignant to me was Meyer's recollection that a resident of a Beijing neighborhood told him, "The Old Quarter is not easy to explain. It's something flowing inside me."

There is a loss of self in relation to others when that *something flowing* is destroyed. It leaves the replaced without context and the replacers with a distorted sense of self. How can we have a relationship with each other if one is forced to leave and the other naturalizes their unwilling absence? Then we don't know the truth about ourselves because we don't know the consequences of our actions on others—and this is the most destructive element, for it denies the fragility of our one and only life.

Instead our lives become overwhelmed by either deprivation or delusion. And those can't be the only choices.

Of course no book on gentrification is complete without a final word from Jane Jacobs, who wrote *Death and Life of Great American Cities* and managed to stop Robert Moses from building a highway through residential Manhattan.

"Fix the buildings," she said. "But leave the people."

And when we don't, we don't know who we are.

Text:	10.75/15 Janson
Display:	Janson MT Pro
Compositor:	Toppan Best-set Premedia Limited
Printer and Binder:	Maple-Vail Book Manufacturing Group